The R
Laura Ingalls

*Who was Real
What was Real in Her
Prairie TV Show*

By Dan L. White

The Real Laura Ingalls

Published by Ashley Preston Publishing
Hartville, Mo. 65667

www.danlwhitebooks.com

Copyright 2013, Dan L. White, all rights reserved.

Cover by Carrie Gaffney; photo from iStock.com.

Little House is a registered trademark of HarperCollins Publishers Inc.

Neither Ed Friendly Productions nor NBC Productions had anything to do with the production of this book.

ISBN 13: 978-1484825181
ISBN 10: 1484825187

Also available in digital format.

Table of Contents

1. Laura Ingalls Did Not Want that There TV Show! 5

2. An Un-Friendly Start to the TV Show 19

3. Big Woods of Wisconsin 35

4. Almanzo's Youth 45

5. The Kansas Prairie 53

6. Walnut Grove 61

7. Silver Lake to Dakota 95

8. The Hard Winter 103

9. Growing Up in the Prairie Town 111

10. Married to Manly 123

11. The First Years of Marriage and After 133

12. Who Wuz and Who Wusin't 141

13. Michael to Laura, Son and Father 169

Endnotes 177

Other Books by Dan L. White 183

Other Books by Dan L. White

Laura Ingalls' Friends Remember Her

Devotionals with Laura

Laura's Love Story: The Lifetime Love of Laura Ingalls and Almanzo Wilder

Laura Ingalls Wilder's Most Inspiring Writings

The Long, Hard Winter of 1880-81: What was it really like?

Big Bible Lessons from Laura Ingalls Little Books

Reading along with Laura Ingalls in the Big Wisconsin Woods

Reading along with Laura Ingalls at her Kansas Prairie Home

The Jubilee Principle: God's Plan for Economic Freedom

Life Lessons from Jane Austen's Pride and Prejudice

Daring to Love like God: Marriage as a Spiritual Union

Wifely Wisdom for Sometimes Foolish Husbands

Homeschool Happenings, Happenstance, and Happiness

Tebow's Homeschooled! Should You?

School Baals: How an old idol with a new name sneaked into your school

Chapter 1

Laura Ingalls Did Not Want That There TV Show!

Isn't this a pretty young lady?

Yes, but don't be misled by her charming appearance. This is the real Laura Ingalls, not the actress who played her on TV, and this real Laura Ingalls did not want the TV show *Little House on the Prairie*.

Can you believe it?

Laura Ingalls, the main character in the series, did not want the TV show *Little House on the Prairie* even to exist!

Laura wrote the book *Little House on the Prairie*, from which the television show was taken. In fact, she wrote a whole series of Little House books that told the story of her life as a young pioneer. That was her personal life, and she was a stubborn stickler for sticking pretty close to the facts.

You see, Laura Ingalls Wilder – the real Laura Ingalls – was feisty.

Okay, Laura Ingalls on the TV show was pretty feisty, too.

We found that out as early as the second episode of the show. Do you remember when Laura and Mary went to school for the first time in Walnut Grove? The first girl they met outside the school was Nellie Oleson. Instead of a friendly "Hi!" Nellie sloughed her shoulders at them and sneered, *"Country girls!"*

You remember that, don't you?

A bit later inside the school, as Laura and Mary were talking to the teacher, Nellie again jeered, *"Country girls!"*

On another day, out in the schoolyard, Nellie pushed Laura and acted like queen of the playground. But –

Laura pushed back, and flat out told Nellie off.

You could tell right then that Noxious Nellie had no idea of the battles that lay ahead with feisty Laura!

You may not have noticed but at the end of that *Country Girls* episode, an airplane can be heard flying overhead at the filming site in California.

That was probably Harriet Oleson, flying in to protect her darling Nellie!

In real life, Nellie and Laura had a few battles, too. Back in 1883, and '84 and '85, week after week on Sunday afternoons, Almanzo took Laura for sleigh rides in winter. Together – just the two of them – they rode a sleek cutter through the snow covered streets of De Smet, South Dakota. In warm weather, they – just the two of them – rode Almanzo's buggy by the twin lakes, Lake Henry and Lake Thompson. Then, one Sunday afternoon, when Laura and Almanzo were going for their customary buggy ride together, somehow Nellie Oleson managed to invite herself along, scrunched down on the buggy seat between Laura and Almanzo!

"*Sunday afternoon,*" Laura wrote in her book *These Happy Golden Years,*" *as she* [Laura] *watched the buggy coming across Big Slough she saw, to her surprise, that someone was with Almanzo. She wondered who it could be, and if perhaps he did not intend to go for a drive that day.*

When the horses stopped at the door, she saw that Nellie Oleson was with him. Without waiting for him to speak, Nellie cried, "Come on, Laura! Come with us for a buggy ride!"

Now isn't that the cat's pajamas? Laura and Almanzo had been riding together for years and suddenly Nellie was in the middle of the seat, inviting Laura to go riding with them!

As Laura sat down –

on the end of the buggy seat, with Nellie in the middle next to Almanzo –

feisty Laura fumed. Nellie was a chatterbox, a blabbermouth, a windbag and a magpie. She talked a lot without saying much. Laura, on the other hand, was spare in her words but rich in her thoughts.

Laura wrote this about Nellie sitting in the middle, between her and Almanzo.

"Laura felt that she was dull company after Nellie's lively chatter, but she was determined that Almanzo would decide that. She would never try to hold him, but no other girl was going to edge her out little by little without his realizing it."[1]

Then Laura did this, about Nellie sitting in the middle, between her and Almanzo.

Almanzo drove horses that were not well broken. Actually, let me restate that – they were half-wild. The slightest scare would send them rearing up and flying across the prairie, dragging the reeling, freewheeling buggy somewhere behind them. Laura was used to that. In fact, she and Almanzo kind of liked riding behind the half-wild horses as they trained them to behave.

However, poor Nellie was afraid of horses.

Did Laura know that?

Somehow, however it came to be, whether happenstance or fate or an act of God –

On that one day when Nellie was sitting between Laura and Almanzo, the dust blanket on Laura's lap somehow managed to flap up into the breeze, fluttering behind the two half-wild horses. How careless of her! That flapping blanket caused the skittish young horses to leap off the ground and start galloping as hard as they could across the prairie!

When those horses jumped, Nellie jumped about as high as they did. Poor little Nellie was scared half to death, and became somewhat aggravated and a bit grouchy, if you can believe it. Consequently, Almanzo learned that Nellie did not really care for half-wild horses the way he did. And Nellie learned that Almanzo did not really care for her, the way she did.

Nellie never went riding with Almanzo and Laura again. All because of that flapping blanket!

On the *Little House on the Prairie* television program, Laura Ingalls was feisty, so you can see the show got that right.

We mentioned Laura's first day of school in Walnut Grove in the TV episode "Country Girls." This is the way the real Laura Ingalls described her first day of school in the town she mostly grew up in, De Smet, South Dakota.

"In front of the schoolhouse strange boys were playing ball, and two strange girls stood on the platform before the entry door.

Laura and Carrie came nearer and nearer. Laura's throat was so choked that she could hardly breathe.

... Then suddenly Laura saw one of the boys spring into the air and catch the ball. He was tall and quick and he moved as beautifully as a

cat. His yellow hair was sun-bleached almost white and his eyes were blue. They saw Laura and opened wide. Then a flashing grin lighted up his whole face and he threw the ball to her.

She saw the ball curving down through the air, coming swiftly. Before she could think, she had made a running leap and caught it.

A great shout went up from the other boys. "Hey, Cap!" they shouted. "Girls don't play ball!"

"I didn't think she'd catch it," Cap answered."[2]

Laura didn't want to catch the ball and act like a tomboy, but when Cap threw it to her, she just couldn't help herself. She made a running leap and – to the amazement of all the boys – caught it!

The real Laura Ingalls even called herself a tomboy.

"I was a regular little tomboy," Laura described herself. *"... I learned to do all kinds of farm work with machinery. I have ridden the binder, driving six horses. And I could ride. I do not wish to appear conceited, but I broke my own ponies to ride. Of course, they were not bad, but they were broncos."*[3]

Laura showed just how spirited she was when she rode a pony for the first time in her life. The Ingalls had just moved to Dakota Territory in 1879 and Laura's cousins offered to let her ride their pony. Laura was twelve but still quite small, so the pony's back was higher than she was. When Laura rode that pony, twice she tumbled off onto the ground. She even bloodied her nose when she banged into the pony's bobbing head. However, Laura remembered that afternoon not for the falls or the bumps, but only as a wonderful time.

That's feisty.

Laura got into a spat with sister Mary that got her spanked by Pa.

"Two little girls had disagreed, as was to be expected because they were so temperamentally different. They wanted to play in different ways, and as they had to play together, all operations were stopped while they argued the question. The elder of the two had a sharp tongue and great facility in using it. The other was slow to speak but quick to act and they both did their best according to their abilities.

Said the first little girl: "You've got a snub nose and your hair is just a common brown color. I heard Aunt Lottie say so! Ah, don't you wish your hair was a b-e-a-u-tiful golden like mine and your nose a fine shape? Cousin Louisa said that about me. I heard her!"

The second little girl could not deny these things. Her dark skin, brown hair, and snub nose, as compared with her sister's lighter coloring and regular features, were a tragedy in her life. She could think of nothing cutting to reply for she was not given to say unkind things nor was her tongue limber enough to say them, so she stood digging her bare toes into the ground, hurt, helpless, and tongue-tied.

The first girl, seeing the effect of her words, talked on. "Besides, you're two years younger than I am, and I know more than you, so you have to mind me and do as I say!"

This was too much! Sister was prettier; no answer could be made to that. She was older, it could not be denied; but that gave her no right to command. At last, here was a chance to act!

"And you have to mind me," repeated the first little girl.

"I will not!" said the second little girl, and then, to show her utter contempt for such authority, this little brown girl slapped her elder, golden-haired sister.

I hate to write the end of the story. No, not the end! No story is ever ended! It goes on and on, and the effect of this one followed this little girl all her life, showing her hatred of injustice. I should say that I dislike to tell what came next, for the golden-haired sister ran crying and told what had happened, except her own part in the quarrel, and the little brown girl was severely punished. To be plain, she was soundly spanked and set in a corner. She did not cry but sat glowering at the parent who punished her and thinking in her rebellious little mind that when she was large enough, she would return the spanking with interest.

It was not the pain of the punishment that hurt so much as the sense of injustice, the knowledge that she had not been treated fairly by one from whom she had the right to expect fair treatment, and that there had been a failure to understand where she had thought a mistake impossible. She had been beaten and bruised by her sister's unkind words and had been unable to reply. She had defended herself in the only way possible for her and felt that she had a perfect right to do so, or if not, then both should have been punished."[4]

Laura wrote that over forty years later. You can tell by reading it that she was a little put out with Pa, and she was still feisty.

Just as in the show, Laura married Almanzo Wilder. They lived on a small farm for fifty-five years and together worked at all the things that small farmers have to do. One of Laura's jobs was to churn the butter. A churn was like a small barrel with a wooden handle sticking out the top and a paddle down in the milk. As Laura moved the handle up and down, the paddle churned the milk and made butter. It was a pretty slow process, though, and took a half hour to an hour for the butter to make.

Almanzo came up with a way that Laura could get her churning done quicker. Laura, though, chucked his new churn out the side door.

"The Man of the Place once bought me a patent churn. "Now," said he, "throw away that old dash churn. This churn will bring the butter in three minutes." It was very kind of him. He had bought the churn to please me and to lighten my work, but I looked upon it with a little suspicion.

There was only one handle to turn and opposite it was a place to attach the power from a small engine. We had no engine, so the churning needed to be done with one hand while the other steadied the churn and held it down. It was hard to do, but the butter did come quickly; and I would have used it anyway because the Man of the Place had been so kind.

The tin paddles which worked the cream were sharp on the edges, and they were attached to the shaft by a screw which was supposed to be loosened to remove the paddles for washing; but I could never loosen it and usually cut my hands on the sharp tin. However, I used the new churn, one hand holding it down to the floor with grim resolution, while the other turned the handle with the strength of despair as the cream thickened. Finally, it seemed that I could use it no longer. "I wish you would bring in my old dash churn," said I to the Man of the Place. "I believe it is easier to use than this after all."

"Oh!" said he, "you can churn in three minutes with this, and the old one takes half a day. Put one end of a board on the churn and the

other on a chair and sit on the board, then you can hold the churn down easily!" And so when I churned I sat on a board in the correct mode for horseback riding and though the churn bucked some, I managed to hold my seat.

"I wish," said I to the Man of the Place, "you would bring in my old dash churn. (It was where I could not get to it.) I cut my hands on these paddles every time I wash them."

"Oh, pshaw!" said he, "you can churn with this churn in three minutes—"

One day when the churn had been particularly annoying and had cut my hand badly, I took the mechanism of the churn – handle, shaft, wheels, and paddles all attached – to the side door which is quite high from the ground and threw it as far as I could. It struck on the handle, rebounded, landed on the paddles, crumpled and lay still – and I went out and kicked it before I picked it up. The handle was broken off, the shaft was bent, and the paddles were a wreck.

"I wish," I remarked casually to the Man of the Place, "that you would bring in my old dash churn. I want to churn this morning."

"Oh, use the churn you have," said he. "You can churn in three minutes with it. What's the use to spend half a day –"

"I can't," I interrupted. "It's broken."

"Why, how did that happen?" he asked.

"I dropped it – just as far as I could," I answered in a small voice, and he replied regretfully, "I wish I had known that you did not want to use it. I would like to have the wheels and shaft, but they're ruined now."

Patient Almanzo and feisty Laura actually made a fine team together. As long as he let her churn the butter her way.

Even after Laura was older and famous for writing the Little House books, she still had a strong will. Travelers often dropped by her house unannounced and banged on her door, just to gawk at the famous writer. Laura didn't like that and often wouldn't even answer the door. Her friend Nava Austin said:

"Laura said that she wanted to be recognized as a person and a friend, not just a celebrity. When she was home, she didn't answer the door unless she was expecting someone or unless they were her friends. She didn't receive people who were just curiosity seekers, because she didn't think they saw her as a real person."[5]

That strong will of Laura Ingalls was combined with strong principles.

"In the house at Rocky Ridge is a rocker where Laura rested and read. After her death, Laura's small Bible was found by the rocker. Inside that Bible were some handwritten notes, listing Laura's favorite Bible selections. Here is what they said.

- *In facing a crisis read 46 Psalm*
- *When discouraged 23 & 24*
- *Lonely or fearful 27*
- *Planning budget St. Luke chapter 19*
- *To live successfully with others read Romans chapter 12*
- *Sick or in pain read 91 Psalm*
- *When you travel carry with you 121 Psalm*
- *When very weary read Matthew 11:28 & 30 and Romans 8:31 to 39*
- *When things are going from bad to worse 2 Timothy 3d*

- When friends go back on you hold to I Corinthians 13th
- For inward peace the 14th chapter of St. John
- To avoid misfortune Matthew 7:24 to 27
- For record for what trust in God can do Hebrews 11
- If you are having to put up a fight – the end of Ephesians
- When you have sinned read I John 3:1 to 21
- And make Psalm 51 your prayer.

Those eighteen sections of the Bible were marked by Laura as being especially valuable. The fact that she did that tells us a lot about her.

What does it tell us?

It tells us that she loved the Bible and placed great value in its teachings. When she marked these eighteen passages, she did not do it for someone else's eyes. These selections were solely for her benefit, for her life and her spiritual needs. At times of distress, despair, or determination, she turned to the Bible, to these passages.

We also know that she knew the Bible well. Her selections are not just from the Psalms or the Gospels, as a Bible dabbler might choose. They go from the middle of the Old Testament all the way to the book of Hebrews, near the end of the New Testament."[6]

So Laura was feisty and a woman of very strong principles. Her first book *Little House in the Big Woods*, published in 1932, was immediately popular. She then had seven more books published over the next eleven years, all of them good sellers. This brought her a certain amount of national fame, which caught the eye of some Hollywood people. A close friend of Laura's, Neta Seal, recalled that Laura was approached about making a movie out of one of her books.

"One time there was some people came down here. It's been several *years ago, of course. And they wanted to make a movie of* The Long Winter. *And she said the way they talked – Well, she didn't much like the way they talked. So she told them that she wouldn't sign any rights for them to make a movie of it, until she read the script that they were going to use.*

When they brought it, she said, "No, I won't sign this. Why have you changed it? This is not like Pa, or our family, or a lot of places."

They said, "We had to change it to make it more interesting."

She said, "No. The children will read my books, and watch this movie, and they won't know which is right. My books are just like I lived them.""[7]

Laura held true to that. She never did allow them to make a Little House movie from her books, because they would not follow the real story.

Isn't that something?

Laura Ingalls Wilder had the chance to have her book made into a Hollywood movie, shown all across America, and that would have made her even more famous and probably would have brought in more money. But she flat turned it down because they didn't get the story right.

Do you know what that means?

That means that Laura would not have let them make a *Little House on the Prairie* television show, either – for the same reason. They changed the story from the way Laura wrote it in her books. Therefore, Laura Ingalls would not have wanted that television show to be made from her books.

Laura died in 1957. Popular television had been around for about a decade. Some of the all time great shows had already appeared, such as *I Love Lucy*, *The Ed Sullivan Show*, and *The Honeymooners*. But Laura never even owned a television! Since she certainly could afford one, that was obviously a deliberate choice on her part. If you visit her home just outside Mansfield, Missouri, which has been left as it was when she died, there is no television set in her home. She did not want a TV!

So Laura would not have allowed the *Little House on the Prairie* show to be made, because it did not strictly follow her books. Furthermore, she didn't even *watch* television herself.

Well, then – how did the show get made, anyway?

Chapter 2

An Un-Friendly Start to the TV Show

Laura Ingalls Wilder would not have allowed a TV show to be made from her books if the story wasn't like her books.

The TV series was not like her books. The scripts did vary from the real story of Laura's life.

Then why is there a *Little House on the Prairie* show?

Because Laura's only little girl did not follow her instructions; and because a couple of little girls loved Laura's books.

Laura and her husband Almanzo Wilder had only one living child, a daughter, Rose, romantically named after the prairie roses that they picked together while they were courting in South Dakota. That one daughter became a nationally famous writer in the first half of the twentieth century.

That's right: Rose – not Laura – was the famous writer! Rose wrote numerous articles for the best-known national magazines, had several commercially successful books, and in the first half of the twentieth century, was one of the highest earning female authors in America.

Rose married Gillette Lane in 1909. She had a little boy about 1910, who died soon after birth. She divorced Lane in 1918, did not remarry and had no more children. Thus, after Rose, there were no further Laura Ingalls Wilder descendants.

It's perfectly natural to leave your estate to your child, and that's just what Laura did in her will. However, since the royalties from the Little House books would continue even after Rose's death, and since Rose herself had no children, Laura added another provision in her will. She stipulated that after Rose's death, ownership of Laura's books would pass to the Wright County Library. Wright County, Missouri is where Laura and Almanzo lived from 1894 until their deaths.

Laura loved her home county. She had a personal involvement with the Wright County Library and used to go there to read western novels! While there, she also visited with the librarian and personal friend Nava Austin. We interviewed Nava for our book *Laura Ingalls' Friends Remember Her*.

"She would read different magazines, and she liked to read paperback westerns," Nava said. *"Laura said to me one time that she didn't want people to know she read that kind of books, the paperback westerns."*[8]

So Laura, who read westerns in the library, left her literary estate to Rose and then, at Rose's death, to the library.

Sometimes people specify life estate in real estate property. Almanzo and Laura did that. They sold their farm but were still allowed to live in the house on the farm as long as either of them was alive. In effect, that's what Laura did with her literary estate. She gave Rose life estate control over the Little House books, but at Rose's death, ownership was to pass to the Wright County Library.

What happened when Laura died?

When Rose gained control of the books, she disagreed with Laura over who should have them next.

In fact, there were many things that Rose did not see Laura's way. Although they were mother and daughter, Laura and Rose were also day and night. They were not at all alike in their views of life. They had very different values.

Laura was a small farm wife who loved the small farm life. She wrote, *"I am thankful for the peacefulness and comparative isolation of country life. This is a happiness which we ought to realize and enjoy.*

She went on, *"We who live in the quiet places have the opportunity to become acquainted with ourselves, to think our own thoughts and live our own lives in a way that is not possible for those who are keeping up with the crowd where there is always something "on for tonight," and who have become so accustomed to crowds that they are dependent upon them for comfort."*[9]

Laura lived near Mansfield, Missouri for sixty-three years and was quite happy with her quiet life there. She loved Wright County, Missouri, as she showed in this 1923 article.

"[A]s we climbed into the hills this side of Springfield, the air grew fresher and more invigorating the farther we went until in Wright county we found the place we were seeking, far enough south so that the winters are mild; high enough for the air to be pure and bracing; sheltered in the hills from the strong winds of the west, yet with little breezes always blowing among them; with plenty of wood for fuel and timber and rocks for building; with low lands for cultivation and upland bluestem pastures for grazing; with game in the woods

and fish in the rivers; and springs of pure, cold, mountain water everywhere.

Here on the very peak of the Ozark watershed are to be found good health, good homes, a good living, good times and good neighbors. What more could anyone want?

Wright county is the highest part of the state south of the Missouri river. Its surface is a broad plateau broken by hills rising from it and by valleys and ravines thru which flow the numerous spring branches, creeks and rivers seeking the waters of the Missouri and the Mississippi.

The rolling hills and fertile valleys are beautifully wooded, except where cleared for agricultural purposes. The trees are of many different kinds, Black oak, White oak, blackjack, maple, cherry, ash, elm, sycamore, gum, hickory, walnut, butternut, persimmon, redbud and linden give great variety to the forest foliage and furnish timber for every use. A peculiarity of the country is that springs break out near the tops of the hills as well as on lower ground and wells of good water on the high lands are only from 40 to 60 feet deep."

That was Laura, happy on her Wright County farm, married to the same man for sixty-four years until his death in 1949, with a very stable and contented life.

Rose, on the other hand, was not at all content to live her life as a small farm wife. She left Mansfield before she was eighteen to work as a telegrapher in Kansas City. That was a bold move for a farm girl to make at that time, living and working on her own in the big city. Later she moved on to Indiana and then California. In California, she sold real estate, got married, then divorced, and soon became a noted writer and world traveler.

Judith Thurman, writing in *The New Yorker* magazine, wrote this about Rose. "*She had lived among bohemians in Paris and Greenwich Village, Soviet peasants and revolutionaries, intellectuals in Weimar Berlin, survivors of the massacres in Armenia, Albanian rebels, and camel-drivers on the road to Baghdad.*" She further said that Rose "*acquired several languages, enjoyed smoking and fornication, and dined at La Rotonde when she wasn't motoring around Europe in her Model T.*"[10]

In a letter, Rose once said this about the people of Laura's Ozarks town. "*People mostly lead such dull lives. It's horrible to contemplate, really, the dullness, the stupidity, of living, for most people. In this little town I see it every time I'm with a group for any length of time, for an afternoon.*"[11]

Can you see any difference between Laura and Rose?

It should come as no great surprise, then, that Rose did not agree with Laura's wishes for the Little House books. In fact, in view of their differences, it might be shocking if Rose had agreed with Laura about her books!

Rose understood marketing much better than Laura did. Rose had regularly sold articles to the leading magazines in America, including *Good Housekeeping*, *Harper's*, *Ladies' Home Journal*, and *The Saturday Evening Post*. She had written biographies of Henry Ford and Herbert Hoover, two of the most famous men in the nation at the time. Rose was one of the most successful women writers, or writers in general, of her time. In 1938 *The Saturday Evening Post* ran her novel *Free Land* in serial form and paid her $30,000, roughly equal to half a million today. Her novel *Let the Hurricane Roar* was made into a nationally broadcast radio drama, starring the famous actress Helen Hayes.

Rose was wealthy and worldly wise but also generous. Generous Rose helped her mother market some of Laura's magazine articles. From 1911 until 1924, Laura regularly wrote articles for the *Missouri Ruralist,* a farm periodical. Those articles were about country living and memories, some of which were included later in her Little House books. *Laura Ingalls Wilder's Most Inspiring Writings* is a sizable collection of forty-eight of the most meaningful of those articles, along with extensive background information concerning her and the times. But writing those magazine articles made Laura very little money. She and Almanzo were small farmers and in need of whatever income they could get, so Rose tried marketing Laura's articles with national magazines that paid more. In 1925, Rose helped Laura place two short articles in the magazine *Country Gentleman,* for which Laura was paid $150 per article. In spite of Rose's efforts, Laura did not become a major magazine author.

Later, Rose helped Laura market the Little House books. Laura wrote her life story originally as *Pioneer Girl*, which covered the period eventually covered by seven different books. No publisher accepted the manuscript. Laura then went to her daughter for help. Rose did help Laura rewrite the material to make it more marketable, and the first book of the series, *Little House in the Big Woods*, was published in 1932. It was an immediate commercial success, even at the very low point of the Great Depression.

After that, Laura didn't need help with marketing.

Or did she?

Laura died in 1957. Rose died eleven years later in 1968. When Rose passed on, she did not leave control of the Little House books to the Wright County Library, as Laura had instructed. Rose left the books to her close associate, Roger Lea MacBride.

Was that nice?

At first that might seem a bit persnickety. Rose deliberately contradicted Laura's will – *purposely disobeyed her mother's last wishes* – and instead left the books to her legal consort, a lawyer yet.

The Wright County Library did not contest the will at the time of Rose's death. They did challenge it legally, nearly twenty years later. It took them a long time to think about it, didn't it? But that may be the way libraries are.

The MacBride family then made a monetary settlement with the library, but retained control of the books. That seems like legal larceny, going directly against the specifics of Laura's last will and testament and getting away with it, but we have to face this question.

What would have happened if the Little House books had been left under the control of the local library?

Well, what usually happens at the local library?

Not much. You sit down, you read a magazine, check out a book, maybe even a western novel. Libraries are quiet, sedate places. They're just libraries, run by –

Librarians!

Librarians have no idea how to market books. They're not supposed to. They only know how to check books out and in, categorize books according to the Dewey Decimal System, and shush noisy kids. They do not know how to make monster marketing deals. They are not media mavens or marketing agents. They're librarians.

Therefore, if Rose had not done what she did, most likely the Little House books would have continued to be popular children's books, having a select appeal –

But remaining unknown to the general population.

Little House on the Prairie would have been no more than a book of juvenile fiction that most people would never have heard of. It would have been on the shelves of nearly every school library in America, but most young people would never have known about it, any more than they know about most of the other books on those shelves.

On the other hand, when Roger Lea MacBride gained control of Laura's literary estate, what happened?

In 1971, he had *The First Four Years* published. That was a manuscript that Laura had written in rough draft form, never finished and never intended to be published. Roger had it published, anyway.

Many people, including me, are glad that he did. Even though the book is not an outstanding work of literature as are Laura's other books, it still tells the continuing story of the people we grew to love in the Little House books. That makes it worthwhile to us.

In 1974, MacBride had *West From Home* published, which is a collection of letters that Laura had written back home to

Almanzo when she visited Rose in San Francisco in 1915. That stack of personal letters is not much of a book.

"I wish I knew how you and Inky were getting along and if Mr. Nall was with you,"[12] Laura wrote in one of those letters. Inky was Laura and Almanzo's dog. Okay, that's not Tom and Huck, just Inky and Mr. Nall. But again I say, people grew to love Laura so much that they constantly seek to know more about her, so they eagerly read a book of letters that she wrote to her hubby when she was on a two month trip.

Yes, Inky was doing all right, in case you're wondering.

In 1962, Rose published a book of Laura's diary entries, written as they traveled from South Dakota to Missouri titled *On the Way Home*. Naturally, when Laura wrote her letters and diary entries, she did not know that someday her private notes and musings would be in books read by people all over the world. She had no inkling that everybody would know exactly what she said about Inky!

As you can see, when Rose and MacBride got control of Laura's books, they made stuff happen. They earned money from the deals, but they helped people become familiar with the books, too.

And in 1974, MacBride made one more deal. He sold the television rights of the Little House literary works to a television producer, Ed Friendly. That turned out to be quite a deal, because it led to making the *Little House on the Prairie* television series.

Could Rose see all of that happening when she left the books to MacBride?

Not exactly, of course. She was smart, but not that smart. Surely she did what she did, though, because she thought it was in the best interest of the books and her mother's literary heritage for MacBride to have control of them, instead of the library. Rose was not just trying to spite Wright County. She was trying to aid her mother's heritage.

Why did TV producer Ed Friendly want to buy the television rights to Little House?

Ed heard from his wife that their daughter loved the Little House books, and Mrs. Friendly encouraged him to make a TV show from them. At first, Ed was not interested. So what if his daughter liked some books? There are a lot of books that people like. Most of them are not TV shows!

Ed noticed, though, that not only had his daughter read Laura Ingalls' books through, she kept reading them – *over and over*. When he saw how really absorbing the books are, then he made the deal to buy the TV rights to them and began to create the TV series.

Friendly asked Michael Landon to direct the pilot movie for *Little House on the Prairie*. They were already acquainted and Ed had been impressed with Michael's directing work. Michael, for his part, had starred in the hit *Bonanza* series for fourteen years. That enormously popular show had run its course and he needed a new direction. After the Bonanza ranch, Little Joe needed a new place to go.

Michael liked the script for the pilot movie well enough. Then guess what?

He, too, learned that his daughter also thought the Little

House books were great. She was hugely excited that her dad might play Pa Ingalls!

How could he say no?

Those two daughters helped motivate their daddies to create the *Little House on the Prairie* show – because of their love for Laura's books!

So Michael agreed to direct the pilot movie – *if* he could play Pa Ingalls.[13]

And that's how Little Joe Cartwright became Pa Ingalls.

The introductory pilot movie was about an hour and a half long. The story stayed fairly close to the story of Laura's book, *Little House on the Prairie*. The Ingalls family left the big woods of Wisconsin to move to the Kansas prairie. On the way, they had to cross a rushing stream that swept their dog Jack away, but he returned to the family a little later. Their neighbor Mr. Edwards helped them celebrate Christmas, and in the spring, a prairie fire raged through their area. At the end of the movie, the government told them that they had to leave the land they had settled on, because it was Indian land.

When the movie aired on NBC on March 30, 1974, it was the highest rated Movie of the Week they had ever shown. With that successful debut, filming then began on the first thirteen episodes of the regular series in June of 1974.[14]

However, the plot of the pilot had already taken up the whole *Little House on the Prairie* book!

How could they make a show from *Little House on the Prairie*, when they had already told the whole story? So when the

Little House on the Prairie television series began, the show did not stick closely to the stories in the books. They made up new stories.

I repeat – when the regular series began, the scripts did not go by the stories in Laura's books. Therefore Laura would not have liked that.

Ed Friendly didn't like it, either.

Melissa Sue Anderson, who played the role of Mary Ingalls in the series, recalled the artistic conflict.

"Ed wanted the shows to follow the story of the books. Michael Landon did not. So after their artistic disagreement, personal relations between Michael Landon and Ed Friendly were a tad less friendly, although Ed never changed his name.

"During the course of the series, this became a major source of conflict between Mike Landon and Ed Friendly, the other executive producer. Ed wanted to stick faithfully, if not slavishly, to the nine Little House books, and the pilot was based on the entire second book: Little House on the Prairie. Mike realized there would not be enough inherent drama if they only used the material in the books and, also, that the characters of Ma and Mary would not be fully fleshed out. He wanted the series to run for several years, at 24 episodes a year. It was a battle Mike Landon and Ed Friendly fought for quite a while."[15]

Perhaps there was also some concern that following the stories of the books would be too depressing, as a short bio of Landon mentions.

"Landon maintained the series would be too dark and depressing

going by the books, and presented in this fashion it would be a turn-off to audiences at home. NBC agreed with Michael's instincts and backed him up."[16]

Actually, an outstanding characteristic about the Little House books is their jollity. That's what Laura's books are – cheerfulness, merriment, and jollity!

However, there are events in her books, taken directly from her actual life history that could have been depressing, if a person was so inclined. Laura and her family moved to Kansas, where Pa built the little log house on the prairie; then they left it after about a year. They lived in Minnesota, in a hole in a creek bank, and their only little boy died and Mary went blind. They moved to South Dakota and the second winter there they almost starved.

All of that could be depressing!

However, Laura was not the type of person to get gloomy. She said this about being cheerful.

"Let's be cheerful! We have no more right to steal the brightness out of the day for our own family than we have to steal the purse of a stranger. Let us be as careful that our homes are furnished with pleasant and happy thoughts as we are that the rugs are the right color and texture and the furniture comfortable and beautiful!"[17]

And from those rough times, this is how the books turned out.

"Pa had tuned his fiddle and now he set it against his shoulder. Overhead the wind went wailing lonely in the cold dark. But in the dugout everything was snug and cosy.

Bits of fire-light came through the seams of the stove and twinkled on Ma's steel knitting needles and tried to catch Pa's elbow. In the shadows the bow was dancing, on the floor Pa's toe was tapping, and the merry music hid the lonely crying of the wind."[18]

Hey – that's not depressing!

The result of the artistic battle between Ed Friendly and Michael Landon?

The decision was made that the *Little House on the Prairie* television series would not go by the stories in Laura's books.

The fact is that it takes a lot of material to make a weekly series. If they covered all of the *Little House on the Prairie* book in the introductory movie, that only left seven books[19] about Laura's life for the rest of the series. The original series ran for eight seasons, plus an additional year under the title *Little House: A New Beginning,* for a total of 203 episodes. If they had stayed with the original story of Laura's life as told in her books, it would have been challenging to stretch it out that far.

Some think the creative decision not to go strictly by Laura's books was a brilliant creative decision. Some think that it was not. Whichever it is, that was the direction the show *Little House on the Prairie* took.

Michael Landon was producer, writer, director and actor in *Little House on the Prairie*. Little Joe from *Bonanza* really grew up when he became Pa Ingalls.

Just as Laura Ingalls Wilder's first book was an immediate success, so the *Little House on the Prairie* television show also was a strong success in its first season in 1974-75, ranking thirteenth among all shows.[20] It remained in the top twenty shows on TV for the next seven seasons, and for two of those years ranked in the top ten.

So then –

We have Laura's beloved books, *Little House on the Prairie* and eight others, which told the true story of her life. And we have the beloved *Little House on the Prairie* television show, which branched off from the story of Laura's life.

Same name. Different stories. In spite of taking different artistic directions, though, they still have much in common, far beyond just having the same title. In fact, there are a number of close connections between the show and the story of Laura's real life.

How much of the show was true? Of all those beloved Little House characters – and a few not so beloved – who was real in Laura's life and who wasn't?

Let's find out.

Chapter 3

Big Woods of Wisconsin

The *Little House on the Prairie* TV series was not like the *Little House on the Prairie* book or Laura Ingalls' other books. The scriptwriters mostly just made their stories up, like writers of any other series. In all of this, Laura Ingalls had three lives. First was her real life. Second was the life she depicted in her books, which was based on her real life but adjusted just a little here and there. Third was her life in the TV series, founded on her life in her books but continued with only a loose correlation.

However, many episodes do connect with Laura's books. We will examine those novels one by one, and highlight the common points between the show and her books, which was the general story of her life.

Laura's first book, *Little House in the Big Woods*, tells of Laura as a four-year-old little girl, in Wisconsin. She called upon her earliest memories and combined them with stories she had heard from her family. Laura actually lived in this little log house in Wisconsin at two different times: first, when she was born when she lived there for a couple of years; second, after they moved back there from Kansas.

Laura was born in 1867, soon after the Civil War ended in 1865.

"I was born in a log house within 4 miles of the legend haunted Lake Pippin in Wisconsin," Laura said. *"I remember seeing deer that my father had killed, hanging in the trees about our forest home. When I was four years old we traveled to the Indian Territory, Fort Scott, Kan., being our nearest town. My childish memories hold the sound of the war whoop and I see pictures of painted Indians."*[21]

In casually writing that article, Laura misstated her age. She was actually two, not four, when they moved to Kansas in 1869. Pa moved to Indian Territory in Kansas because he had heard that the US government would soon open the land to homesteader settlement. He wanted to be first in line to get a free farm in rich country.

Laura was certainly too young to remember anything about living in Wisconsin before they went to Kansas, but they moved back there in 1871, when she was four. For three more years they lived in the same little log house as before, until Laura was seven. Those memories and the memories of her parents and sisters are told in the *Little House in the Big Woods* story.

The Ingalls family in the big woods book was Ma and Pa, Laura and her sister Mary, two years older than Laura. Their log cabin in the woods was a few miles east of the Mississippi River near the village of Pepin and close to Grandpas and Grandmas and uncles and aunts and cousins. The family stories that Laura included told of such things as Pa killing a bear; Ma petting a bear – accidentally, of course; of Pa running from a screech owl; and Grandpa running from a panther.

The stories, as you can tell, are mild. There is no violence in the book and no vulgarities whatsoever. Actually, there is not even so much as a harsh word. The plot is just barely there – it is a children's book, after all – and this is the least developed of the finished novels. Yet when *Little House in the Big Woods* appeared in 1932 at the depth of the Great Depression, the novel was immediately popular. The reviewers said that it sounded real, not made up. It has never gone out of print since.

This book set the tone for all of Laura Ingalls' books: interesting, happy, inspiring, and real.

Like her.

In a magazine article written in 1917, Laura wrote, *"We all know there is a spirit in every home, a sort of composite spirit composed of the thoughts and feelings of the members of the family as a composite photograph is formed of the features of different individuals. This spirit meets us at the door as we enter the home. Sometimes it is a friendly, hospitable spirit and sometimes it is a cold and forbidding."*

"Let us be as careful that our homes are furnished with pleasant and happy thoughts as we are that the rugs are the right color and texture and the furniture comfortable and beautiful."[22]

Laura and her husband Almanzo indeed furnished their home with pleasant and happy thoughts. This is how Laura recalled an evening with her good friends in that room.

"A group of friends was gathered around a glowing fire the other evening. The cold outside and the warmth and cheer and soft lights

within had opened their hearts and they were talking freely together as good friends should.

"I propose that we eliminate the word can't from our vocabularies for the coming year," said Mrs. Betty. "There ain't no such animile anyhow."

"But sometimes we just c—" began Sister Sue, then stopped abruptly at the sound of an amused chuckle.

"Oh, well—if you feel that way about it!" rejoined Mrs. Betty, "but I still insist that if you see such an animal it is only a creature of the imagination. When I went to school they tried to teach me that it was noble to say, 'I'll try' when confronted with a difficult thing to be done, but it always sounded weak to me. Why! the very expression presupposes failure," she went on with growing earnestness. "Why not say I will, and then make good? One can, you know, for if there is not one way to do a thing there are usually two."

"That word 'can't' with its suggestion of failure!" exclaimed George. "Do you know a man came up to me on the street the other day and said, "You can't lend me a dollar, can you?" He expected to fail in his request—and he most certainly did," he added grimly.

"After all," said brother James slowly, "people do a good deal as they are expected to do, even to saying the things they are expected to say. the power of suggestion is very strong. Did you ever notice how everyone will agree with you on the weather? I have tried it out many a time just for fun. Before the days of motor cars, when we could speak as we passed driving along the road, I have said to the first man I met, 'This is a fine day,' and regardless of what the weather might be, he never would fail to answer, 'Sure, it's a fine day,' or something to that effect and pass on smiling. To the next man I met I would say, 'Cold weather we're having,' and his reply would always be, 'Coldest I ever knew at this season,' or 'Mighty cold this morning,' and he would go on his way shivering. No matter if it's raining a man usually will agree with you that it's awfully dry weather, if you suggest it to him right."

"Speaking of friends," said Philip, which no one had been doing tho all could trace the connecting thought, "Speaking of friends—I heard a man say not long ago that he could count all the friends he had on the fingers of one hand. I wonder"—and his voice trailed off into silence as his thought carried him away. A chorus of protest arose.

"Oh, how awful!" exclaimed Pansy, with the tender eyes. "Anyone has more friends than that. Why, if everybody is sick or in trouble everybody is his friend."

"It all depends on one's definition of friend," said Mrs. Betty in a considering tone. "What do we mean when we say 'friend'? What is the test for a friend?" A silence fell upon the little group around the glowing fire.

"But I want to know," insisted Mrs. Betty. "What is the test for a friend? Just what do you mean Philip, when you say, 'He is my friend'?"

"Well, "Philip replied, "when a man is my friend I expect he will stand by me in trouble, that he will do whatever he can do to help me if I am needing help and do it at once even at cost of inconvenience to himself."

"Now, Pansy! How do you know your friends?" still insisted Mrs. Betty.

"My friends," said Pansy, with the tender eyes, "will like me anyway, no matter what my faults are. They will let me do as I *please and not try to change me but will be my friends whatever I do."*

"Next," began Mrs. Betty, but there were exclamations from every side. "No! No! It's your turn now! We want to know what your test of friendship is!"

"Why! I was just asking for information," answered Mrs. Betty with a brilliant smile, the warmth of which included the whole circle. "I wanted to know—"

"Tell us! Tell us!" they all insisted.

"Well, then," earnestly, "my friends will stand by me in trouble. They will love me even tho I make mistakes and in spite of my faults, but if they see me in danger of taking the wrong course they will warn me. If necessary, they will even tell me of a fault which perhaps is growing on me unaware. One should dare anything for a friend, you know."

"Yes, but to tell friends of a fault is dangerous," said gentle Rosemary. "It is so likely to make them angry."

"To be sure," Mrs. Betty answered. "But if we are a friend we will take it thankfully for the sake of the spirit in which it is given as we do a Christmas present which otherwise we would not care for."

> "Remember well and bear in mind
> A constant friend is hard to find
> And when you find one good and true
> Change not the old one for the new."

quoted Philip as the group began to break up.

"No, don't change 'em," said George, in the bustle of the putting on of wraps. "Don't change 'em! Just take 'em all in!"[23]

Little House in the Big Woods is simpler than the other books, since Laura was such a little girl at that time. As little Laura grew up in the books, the writer Laura also grew in her writing. But one thing never changed – all her books were furnished with her happy, friendly spirit.

Little House in the Big Woods ends this way.

"Laura," Pa said. "Go to sleep, now."

But Laura lay awake a little while, listening to Pa's fiddle softly playing and to the lonely sound of the wind in the Big Woods. She looked at Pa sitting on the bench by the hearth, the fire-light gleaming on his brown hair and beard and glistening on the honey-brown fiddle. She looked at Ma, gently rocking and knitting.

She thought to herself, "This is now." She was glad that the cosy house, and Pa and Ma and the fire-light and the music, were now. They could not be forgotten, she thought, because now is now. It can never be a long time ago."

Pa Ingalls was a dedicated fiddle player and he fiddled warm music throughout Laura's books, except for the last one where she was married. The television series did picture Pa as a fiddle player. In episode 5, "The Love of Johnny Johnson," Pa played a fast fiddle tune early in the show, and then toward the end, he fiddled a song that was guaranteed to put Carrie to sleep.[21] The book, though, emphasize Pa's fiddling even more than the show does, where his merry music is a focal point for the family's happiness.

Laura obviously loved Pa's fiddling, to have emphasized it in the books as she did. When they all got older. Pa wanted Laura to have his beloved fiddle. As Laura was leaving to move to their new Missouri home, Pa made this speech to the family.

"Laura, you've always stood by us, from the time you was a little girl knee-high to a grasshopper. Your Ma and I have never been able to do as much for you girls as we'd like to. But there'll be a little something left when we're gone, and, I hope, I want to say now, I want you all to witness, when the time comes, Laura, I want you to have the fiddle."

Then, according to daughter Rose, Laura said this. "To think, Manly, he gave me the fiddle.... It's the first thing I remember, Pa's playing us to sleep.... by the campfires ... all the way out here.... I see it now, though I didn't then—we never could have gotten through it all without Pa's fiddle."[25]

Laura did inherit Pa's fiddle, which is now on display at her home in Mansfield, Missouri. To pay tribute to its most notable citizen, the town celebrates an annual Wilder Days festival.

"Welcome to "Wilder Days – Mansfield Missouri

On the 3rd weekend in September, people who love the Little House Books and other memories of Laura Ingalls Wilder come to Mansfield, Missouri to celebrate together and to commemorate the woman who wrote of pioneer history. Her stories of real life in the 19th century have entranced readers and have inspired films for television and theater...

The weekend is as full as we can make it. Favorite activities include Look-A-Like contests for Little Laura and Little Farmer Boy, games and activities for kids and grown-ups, demonstrations of lost arts, FOOD, vendors for almost everything you can imagine, a huge *parade, quilt shows, mechanical shows that feature vintage equipment, tools and cars, musical entertainment from local groups and more."*[26]

And during that festival, Pa's fiddle is often played.

When they lived in Wisconsin, Laura's age was birth to two and four to seven. In the book *Little House in the Big Woods*, Laura pictured herself as being four, so she was younger in this book than in the TV series.

The "Journey in the Spring" two-part episode tied in with the Wisconsin woods. Charles received word that his mother had died back in Wisconsin, so he traveled there to be with his father, Lansford Ingalls. In the big woods, Charles visited with his brother Peter Ingalls and his wife Eliza Quiner Ingalls, Caroline's sister. Charles brought his pa back to live with him and Caroline in Walnut Grove, and after spending some time with them, Lansford returned to his home in the big woods.

Sure enough, Charles' father was Lansford Ingalls, and he did have a brother Peter, and Caroline did have a sister Eliza Quiner, and those two brothers did marry those two sisters.[27] "Journey in the Spring" was a very moving episode, and even though Laura did have a grandfather Lansford, she did not write such a story of him.

"Going Home," the last show of the second season, was about Charles' plan to return to the big woods of Wisconsin. The Ingalls had a bumper crop ready to harvest, but a tornado destroyed it. Charles was so discouraged that he announced that he was giving up on Walnut Grove and the family was moving back to Wisconsin where they came from. Caroline and the girls helped restore Pa's spirits, and they decided to stay in Walnut Grove and rebuild their lives there.

In real life, Charles did move back to Wisconsin from Kansas. Later they moved on to Walnut Grove, Minnesota. The real Charles Ingalls was never one for staying put, though. He left Walnut Grove for Iowa, then back to Walnut Grove, then on farther west. They moved to De Smet, South Dakota, which, before statehood and combined with North Dakota, was Dakota Territory. Even when they were settled in De Smet, Pa still wanted to go even farther west. Caroline finally would not agree to another move, so they spent the rest of their lives in De Smet, where they died and are buried.

That Little House episode taught the value of not giving up, of not complaining and of making the best of life, and although Laura did not write that particular story, her books were chock full of that kind of thinking.

Chapter 4

Almanzo's Youth

Laura's second book, published in 1933, wasn't about Laura at all. The follow up to her successful big woods book was *Farmer Boy*, the story of Almanzo Wilder's boyhood in New York State.

First of all, you may wonder where in the world such a name came from. Some names from long ago seem different to us, like Hortense or Horatio, but Almanzo's name was kind of created out of the blue.

In Laura's book *Little Town on the Prairie*, Almanzo gave Laura his name card; name cards were a fad back then in the early 1880's. Naturally his name card had his name, Almanzo, on it.

"It's kind of an outlandish name," he said. Laura tried to think of something nice to say about it. She said, "It is quite unusual."

"It was wished on me," he said grimly. "My folks have got a notion there always has to be an Almanzo in the family, because 'way back in the time of the Crusades there was a Wilder went to them, and an Arab or somebody saved his life. El Manzoor, the name was. They changed it after a while in England, but I guess there's no way to improve it much."

"I think it is a very interesting name," said Laura honestly."[28]

Wasn't she nice?

El Manzoor, or Almanzo, grew up on his family's farm in upstate New York. *Farmer Boy* was set in 1866, when Almanzo was turning nine years old. The book shows him planting and weeding, training calves and harrowing with a team of horses at nine years of age, and liking all of that better than going to school.

"It was January in northern New York State, sixty-seven years ago. Snow lay deep everywhere. It loaded the bare limbs of oaks and maples and beeches, it bent the green boughs of cedars and spruces down into the drifts. Billows of snow covered the fields and the stone fences.

Down a long road through the woods a little boy trudged to school, with his big brother Royal and his two sisters, Eliza Jane and Alice. Royal was thirteen years old, Eliza Jane was twelve, and Alice was ten. Almanzo was the youngest of all, and this was his first going-to-school, because he was not quite nine years old.

He had to walk fast to keep up with the others, and he had to carry the dinner-pail.

"Royal ought to carry it," he said. "He's bigger than I be."

Royal strode ahead, big and manly in boots, and Eliza Jane said:

"No, 'Manzo. It's your turn to carry it now, because you're the littlest."

Eliza Jane was bossy. She always knew what was best to do, and she made Almanzo and Alice do it."[29]

In 1920, Laura recorded Almanzo's memories of his boyhood on his parents' farm in this magazine article.

"I never realized how much work my father did. Why, one winter he sorted 500 bushels of potatoes after supper by lantern light. He sold them for $1.50 a bushel in the spring, too, but he must have got blamed tired of sorting potatoes down cellar every night until he had handled more than 500 bushels of them."

"What did your mother do while your father was sorting potatoes?" I asked.

"Oh, she sewed and knit," said The Man of The Place. "She made all our clothes, coats and pants, undergarments for father and us boys as well as everything she and the girls wore, and she knit all our socks and mittens—shag mittens for the men folks, do you remember, all fuzzy on the outside? She didn't have time enough in the day to do all the work and so she sewed and knit at night."

"Mother did all her sewing by hand then," he said, "and she spun her own yarn and wove her own cloth. Father harvested his grain by hand with a sickle and cut his hay with a scythe. I do wonder how he ever got it done."[30]

Almanzo learned well from his parents and was a terrific worker himself, accomplishing some things that make us wonder how *he* got it done. In the winter of 1894-95, Almanzo and Laura cleared about twenty acres of woods on their Mansfield farm, to plant apple trees there come spring. She was a petite little lady and he was recovering from a possible stroke, but the two of them cleared half their "farm" with hand tools, so that was quite an accomplishment.

Almanzo Wilder as a young man.

Almanzo was a cheerful person, affable and jovial; he just laughed a lot. I asked a friend of Laura and Almanzo's, Peggy Dennis, what he was like.

"Now Almanzo was a cut up and he was witty.

It was almost like he was club footed. He had the front of his shoe leather sewn way back and I think he did it himself. They said they thought he had suffered a stroke at one time. He always carried a heavy cane.

Almanzo had a big white mustache and it looked like he had a stern look, like he was frowning. If you just looked at him, you might think that he was kind of mean. But he was a cut up. He was always clowning with my mother.

I asked Peggy to give us an example.

"Well, one time he came into the market and my mother pretended she didn't see him. So he took his big heavy cane and rapped hard on the counter. She turned around and said, "Oh, I didn't see you." He knew she was teasing him and he thought that was real funny."[31]

The actor who portrayed Almanzo on the television series, Dean Butler, was rather tall and handsome. That probably had a lot to do with him being picked for the part. The real Almanzo was not a bad looking fellow in his youth, but he was not tall at all. It is said that Laura was an inch under five feet tall and when Almanzo stood next to her, he was only a few inches taller.

Dean was so unfamiliar with the Little House books that he had never even heard of Laura.

"Before being hired to play Almanzo Wilder on the "Little House" series I had never read any of the "Little House" books and to be honest I had never heard of Laura Ingalls Wilder,"[32] Butler admitted in an interview. He thought that was probably a good thing, saying that *"it's fortunate that I had no deep knowledge of the books so I didn't have to worry about living up to Laura's books."*

The real Almanzo was a terrific horseman. *Farmer Boy* showed in great detail his love for horses. He lived through the transition from old time horsepower to modern horsepower, as we talked about in *Laura Ingalls Wilder's Most Inspiring Writings*.

"Almanzo was an expert with horses. He saw the change in the value of a horse, as horses were replaced on the roads by cars and on the farms by tractors.

He personally experienced that change and it must have been hard, in more ways than one. In 1925, Rose bought her parents a Buick. Once, when she was teaching Almanzo, the horseman, how to drive the motorcar, Almanzo was driving, a couple of cars were coming in the other direction, and he wanted to slow down.

If you're used to driving a team of horses and you want to slow down, what do you do?

Farmer Boy braced his feet against the floorboard, pulled back hard on the steering wheel and yelled –

"Whoa!"

There were a couple of problems with that. One was that when he yelled "Whoa!" the Buick totally ignored him.

The second was that when he braced himself and pulled back, his foot was on the gas pedal.

The net result of it all was that the car did not go whoa but spurted ahead, out of the road and into an oak tree. Only then did the headstrong Buick obey Almanzo's command.

That was a bit of a bump, at least on Rose's head, but Almanzo did learn to drive a car. Laura did, too, but then left the driving to the Man of the Place.

Almanzo was sixty-eight when he learned to drive a car, and he must have felt a bit outdated. As did all the horses who were put out to pasture when cars and tractors came in, as relics of a bygone time, even though they knew what "Whoa!" meant."[33]

Next to Laura and daughter Rose, horses were the love of Almanzo's life. He worked with horses from the time he was a boy and plowed with a team when he was the age of a modern fourth-grader. On the other hand, Dean Butler, the onscreen Almanzo, had a lot to learn about horses. He recalled his debut on the show when, *"on my first day I nearly killed a horse when the buckboard team got away from me during my first shot."*

Although the books had Almanzo as six years older than Laura, he was actually ten years older. When he first showed an interest in her, she was about fifteen and he was a grown man in his mid-twenties. The TV series depicted that age difference well. Butler was actually eight years older than Melissa Gilbert, who played Laura. *"I was 23 when I met Melissa,"* Butler said. *"She was 15. 8 years difference at that stage of life was huge."*

The real Laura Ingalls had trouble accepting the fact that a man so much older than her was really trying to court her. On the show, the age difference also caused some pauses for Dean and Melissa. *"I'd had a number of girlfriends...I had been in love. Melissa and I had very little in common other than a desire, which we rarely verbalized to each other, to do the best job we could creating the relationship between Laura and Almanzo. Sometimes it was difficult but we made it work more often than not."*

Laura and Almanzo's marriage lasted from 1885 until his death in 1949. As you can tell from the length of their marriage, their love was strong and enduring. The prologue to our book *Laura's Love Story* talks about that romance.

"Truth is stranger than fiction, the saying goes. And real life love is sometimes stronger than the romance of fiction.

The romance of fiction is filled with fire and flames and quick passing passion. The romance of real life is filled with the lifetimes of two people, who have never known any other and never wanted to; who love not just during the best of times, but also the worst of times; who love the pretty young lass or handsome lad and the aged octogenarian. This is not a love that flees quickly, but one that lasts as long as the lovers themselves. This is the greatest of loves, the fire that cannot be quenched, the feeling that time does not fade.

Laura Ingalls and Almanzo Wilder had such a love. This is their story: not so much the story of their lives, which has often been told, but the story of their love, which has seldom been noted. Their love story has the beauty of a fairy tale; if not the part about the prince and princess, then certainly the part about living happily ever after."[34]

So when the show portrayed Laura and Almanzo in love, they certainly got that right. In the television series, Laura called him Manly instead of Almanzo, and in fact, that is what Laura called her El Manzoor in real life.

Farmer Boy was written in the same cheery style as Laura's other books, but the TV show was about Laura's youth, not Almanzo's, so the show did not take episodes from that book. Perhaps at some point someone will make a show from it. What the series did get right is that Almanzo was Laura's beau, and they had a beau-tiful love story.

Chapter 5

The Kansas Prairie

Little House on the Prairie!

That is Laura's third book, that is the title chosen for the TV series, and that is the phrase most connected with Laura Ingalls.

The show's locale is supposed to be Minnesota, the series was actually filmed in California, and the *Little House on the Prairie* book was set in Kansas. With such a geographically varied base, no wonder the show is a worldwide hit!

In Kansas, the Ingalls settled only about ten miles north of Oklahoma, which is a much warmer climate than Wisconsin. The Ingalls' Kansas home was just two hundred miles due west of Laura's eventual last little house in Mansfield, Missouri. Little did little Laura know when she was in Kansas that she was so close to her beloved Rocky Ridge Farm.

The *Little House on the Prairie* novel opens with the Ingalls leaving the big woods of Wisconsin and traveling to Kansas in their covered wagon.

"A long time ago, when all the grandfathers and grandmothers of today were little boys and little girls or very small babies, or perhaps

not even born, Pa and Ma and Mary and Laura and Baby Carrie left their little house in the Big Woods of Wisconsin. They drove away and left it lonely and empty in the clearing among the big trees, and they never saw that little house again. They were going to the Indian country. Pa said there were too many people in the Big Woods now."[35]

In the spring of 1869, the Ingalls settled about thirteen miles south of Independence, Kansas, in what was still Osage Indian territory. There Pa Ingalls built a log cabin and hand dug a well, trying to establish a homestead on land that he thought would soon be opened for homesteading.

On August 3 of 1870, Laura's sister Carrie was born in Kansas. Laura included Carrie in her first book, *Little House in the Big Woods*, referring to her as baby Carrie. The first time Laura lived in Wisconsin, Carrie hadn't even been born. The second time she lived there, Carrie was indeed baby Carrie, or maybe toddler Carrie.

You may be asking an obvious question. Since Laura adjusted the facts of her life in her books, how could she complain about others changing things for movies? Perhaps it has to do with the degree of the changes. *"Although Laura often changed details to better fit the voice of a children's author, all of her books were based on her recollections,"* says New World Encyclopedia. *"Characters were based on childhood siblings and friends; stories reflected everyday chores and family togetherness through both mundane and adverse times."*[36]

Carrie Ingalls was about three years younger than Laura, and was depicted in the books as having the weakest health of any in the Ingalls family. However, like Laura, she sounds like a feisty lady.

Carrie lived most of her adult life in Keystone, South Dakota. The Keystone Chamber of Commerce says, *"At nineteen years of age, Carrie was an apprentice on the Leader staff, the town's weekly newspaper. She learned all aspects of the newspaper business. The Leader was eventually combined with the De Smet News and she may have worked for the rival Kingsbury Independent. Carrie worked in the newspaper business for about five years in De Smet. She also clerked in stores, did substitute teaching and worked in the Post Office. At thirty-five years of age, Carrie went to Boulder, Colorado in search of a climate that would clear her sinus and asthma problems."*[37]

Pa Ingalls had proven up on a homestead claim near De Smet, South Dakota, so about a quarter century later, Carrie also took out a claim. *"The U.S. government opened various Indian lands to white settlers. Lucky white men and women would win the right to homestead in the Indian lands by lottery. Carrie decided to throw her name into the hat and she won. The homestead claim was near the town of Topbar, north of Philip, South Dakota. She lived in a tiny tar-paper shanty which was typical of that day, living on the homestead for at least six months each year and the remainder of the time in De Smet."*[38]

Like her sister Laura, apparently Carrie had a way with words, and wound up in the newspaper business.

"Carrie would eventually meet E. L. Senn who was known as the "Final Proof King of South Dakota." It was reported that Senn owned as many as fifty-one newspapers in South Dakota. Fundamentally, Senn made his money because each homesteader had to file final proof sheets for five consecutive weeks. According to a government ruling, such newspapers were to be paid five dollars by the landholder for each final proof published, and any contestant to a

settler's right to the land must pay a publication fee. Carrie first worked for E.L. Senn in the town of Pedro, not too far from her claim. By the summer of 1909, Carrie was the manager working for Senn at the Pedro Bugle."

Eventually, in 1911, Carrie arrived in the gold mining town of Keystone, South Dakota to run the newspaper there. At that time, Carrie was forty years old and had never married.

Then she met a gold miner.

The Roosevelt Inn History, Roosevelt Inn being a hotel in Keystone, says, *"The first building on the site -- a miner's shack -- was built by an old-time gold prospector named Dave Swanzey, who staked out a placer claim along Grizzly Creek.*

Dave wasn't too lucky in finding gold -- the big strike was two miles downstream at the Keystone Mine -- but he did gain some fame in his own right as the man who gave Mt. Rushmore its name. Later, Dave married Carrie Ingalls, the sister of Laura Ingalls Wilder, the author of "Little House on the Prairie." Dave and Carrie lived in a cabin downstream from where the Roosevelt Inn sits today. There's a plaque in Keystone near where their cabin used to be."[39]

So Dave didn't find a lot of gold but he did find Carrie Ingalls. Carrie and David were married in 1912. He was a widower with two children, Mary, eight, and Harold, six. Carrie was already forty-one at the time of her wedding, and she and David never had children, so Carrie raised his two children as her own.

Years ago, I talked with a friend of Laura's, Neta Seal, who had gone with her to visit Carrie in the spring of 1939. I asked Neta, *"On the trip, did Laura talk about the Ingalls family much?"*

Neta answered, *"She would talk about her mother and father some, but not too much. She talked about Carrie. Carrie's husband had died and he had left her a gold mine. That was when the government wouldn't let them mine, and she didn't even have enough money to pay her taxes. Mrs. Wilder paid her taxes."*

Carrie and Dave's home town of Keystone, South Dakota is where Mt. Rushmore is located. When the sculptor Gutzon Borglum visited that area looking for a suitable mountain for the memorial, David Swanzey was among the men who showed Borglum the mountain that eventually became the site. Harold Swanzey, the boy that Carrie raised as her own, helped Borglum with the work. Millions of people have visited Mt. Rushmore and gazed at the stony faces of Washington, Jefferson, Theodore Roosevelt and Lincoln. Many of those people were also *Little House on the Prairie* fans, but few knew beforehand that Carrie Ingalls' family was connected with that famous landmark.[40]

Carrie Ingalls

In the television series, identical twins Lindsay and Sidney Greenbush, played Carrie Ingalls. They took turns playing the part. In one episode, though, both twins appeared onscreen at the same time. That episode was "The Godsister," first shown on December 18, 1978. Pa Ingalls had left home for a month to work away from Walnut Grove. Carrie was lonely and created an imaginary friend, who looked just like her. And in that show, both twins acted at the same time.[41]

When the *Little House on the Prairie* show ended, most of the Greenbush twins' acting was behind them. Lindsay became a boxer – doesn't that knock you out? – and personal trainer in California. Sidney married a horse breeder in California, William Foster. She was married to him for nine years, until he took his own life at age 55. It was reported that two days before Foster committed suicide, Sidney informed him that she wanted a divorce. *"The police report states that Foster called Greenbush -- who he referred to as his "ex-wife" -- to tell her of his suicidal thoughts. Greenbush then called the police, but by the time they arrived, Foster had already shot himself."*[42]

In the *Little House on the Prairie* book, Ma helped Pa build their log cabin in Kansas, but she was hurt when a log fell on her foot. Then Charles discovered that they had a bachelor neighbor who was only two miles away. He and Pa traded work, and the fellow came over to help Pa build the log house.

"Early next morning Mr. Edwards came. He was lean and tall and brown. He bowed to Ma and called her "Ma'am," politely. But he told Laura that he was a wildcat from Tennessee. He wore tall boots and a ragged jumper, and a coonskin cap, and he could spit tobacco juice farther than Laura had ever imagined that anyone could spit tobacco juice. He could hit anything he spit at, too. Laura tried and

tried, but she could never spit so far or so well as Mr. Edwards could."[43]

That was Mr. Edwards' introduction in Laura's books.

In the television series, Mr. Edwards was one of the most beloved characters. Isaiah Edwards, played by Victor French, appeared in about a third of the episodes. Up until that series, French had often played bad guys in westerns, but after *Little House on the Prairie*, he was one of the most beloved characters on TV. He left the series for a couple of years to star in his own situation comedy called *Carter Country*. When that series ended, he again appeared in Little House. He and Michael Landon were close personal friends and they worked very well together onscreen. After Little House, Victor starred with Michael Landon in *Highway to Heaven*, and actually worked in more shows in that series than in the Little House series.

In the series episode "A Christmas They Never Forgot," shown right before Christmas in 1981, Mary and her husband Adam Kendall returned to Walnut Grove for Christmas, just as a blizzard struck. During that snowed in Christmas Eve, Laura told the story of the Christmas in Kansas when Mr. Edwards came to visit.

This is how Laura described that visit in the *Little House on the Prairie* book.

"Great fishhooks, Edwards! Come in, man!

What's happened?" Pa exclaimed.

Laura saw the stockings limply dangling, and she scrooged her shut eyes into the pillow. She heard Pa piling wood on the fire, and she heard Mr. Edwards say he had carried his clothes on his head when he swam the creek. His teeth rattled and his voice shivered. He would be all right, he said, as soon as he got warm.

"It was too big a risk, Edwards," Pa said. "We're glad you're here, but that was too big a risk for a Christmas dinner."

"Your little ones had to have a Christmas," Mr. Edwards replied. "No creek could stop me, after I fetched them their gifts from Independence."[44]

Mr. Edwards does not play nearly so large a role in the books as in the show, although he is a beloved character in his limited appearances.

After the Ingalls arrived in Kansas in 1869, they built a log cabin and the next year put out a garden; they were well on the way to making a homestead. However, the land was still Osage land. Pa heard that the United States Army was going to evict white settlers from the Indian land, so in the spring of 1871, Pa moved his family back to Wisconsin.

In fact, later that year the Osage sold their land to the United States and then it was opened up for homesteading. Pa Ingalls was right in his original belief that the area would be homesteaded. He was just a little too early in his timing. The man who had bought the Ingalls farm in Wisconsin let it go back to them, so in the spring of 1871, two years after arriving in Kansas, the Ingalls loaded up their covered wagon again and made the long trip back to the Big Woods. The little house on the Kansas prairie was undoubtedly lived in by the next settlers who came to that spot, and that became their homestead. If only Pa had known.

Chapter 6

Walnut Grove

Which one of Laura's books is most like the *Little House on the Prairie* TV show?

That's not *Little House on the Prairie*, but *On the Banks of Plum Creek*?

That's right. The series has the same name as the *Little House on the Prairie* book, but has most in common with *On the Banks of Plum Creek*. In the first episode of the show, the Ingalls family settled on Plum Creek near the town of Walnut Grove, Minnesota, as in the Plum Creek book. The rest of the story in episode one, though, was not.

When the Ingalls lived on the banks of Plum Creek, they actually lived in a bank of Plum Creek.

Where the bank rose up and made a dirt wall beside the creek, someone had dug a hole in the bank. In front of that hole was a wall built out of strips of prairie sod stacked tightly together. The sod wall had a wooden door and a window, which was covered not with costly glass, but with greased paper, to let just a little light shine through. The roof was wiry willow branches woven together so closely that a person could stand on it. Hay was then piled on top of and tucked in between the willow branches, to keep out almost all of the rain. A stovepipe stuck up through that au natural roof.

The creek bank house had only one room. The floor was brown dirt and the walls were dirt, too, but they had been whitewashed with lime, to add a touch of brightness to the dark, earthy room. Caroline Ingalls took a willow twig broom and brushed the loose dirt down from the walls, so that it wouldn't fall on them as they sat in their house. She did not try to sweep the dirt from the floor.

Their house was called a dugout, because it was just a hole dug out in a steep bank. On the unsettled prairie in the times soon after the Civil War, new settlers made houses out of boards, which were expensive and hard to get; out of sod, which was warm but took a lot of work to build; and sometimes out of holes in the ground, which was very warm, but kinda dark, dank and dirty.

Caroline Ingalls as a young wife and mother.

When the Ingalls moved into their dugout, flowers and grass grew on the bank all around their house, on the front wall of their house, and even on the roof of their house. As Ma Ingalls might say, "Every cloud has a silver lining," and the silver lining of the dugout was its decorative floral exterior.

Charles Ingalls traded a team of horses for the farm with the dugout and a couple of oxen. The man who lived in the dugout wanted to get out and go farther west. He was Norwegian and his name was Mr. Hanson.

In the television series, Lars Hanson appears in the very first regular episode. In the show, he owned a lumber mill in Walnut Grove and was the closest thing that the small town had to a tycoon. He is a recurring character in the series, but in the book, Mr. Hanson was not. Once he traded the farm to the Ingalls, he was never heard from again.

Of course, Walnut Grove is the setting of the TV series, although the show wasn't actually filmed there. The Ingalls farm was actually about three miles north of Walnut Grove, Minnesota. The first settlers in the real town of Walnut Grove lived in a grove of black walnut trees, giving the town its name. More settlers came in when the railroad built by the town in 1872. Walnut Grove established a post office in 1873, and Lafayette Bedal served as its first postmaster. The plat of Walnut Grove as a town was filed on September 10, 1874.[45]

The present town of Walnut Grove is proud of its history, which it recalls in this way.

"The community of Walnut Grove began in 1870. The 1870's were exciting times. A nation, fresh from civil war, had literally been ripped apart. Its citizens sought new beginnings far from the settled

eastern states. The Homestead Act of 1862 urged pioneers, sodbusters and immigrants to 'head west' and make their mark on the great expanse of the Plains. It was a time of change and progress in communications and travel. A telegraph system joined the country from coast to coast in 1861. East and West were joined by rail in 1869.

During the 1870's, the village of Walnut Grove grew. Pioneers settled along the banks of Plum Creek. The land was rich and game was plentiful. Hardships were common on the prairie. A grasshopper plague almost destroyed the settlement in the 1870's. Perseverance, hard work, and a strong Christian faith carried the community through the many hard times."

Lafayette Bedal, the village's first postmaster, opened his home to the children in 1873 conducting school classes in his living room. The Congregational Church was built in the village in 1874. Other buildings included: three general stores, hardware, drug, grocery, flour mill, feed stores, hotel, confectionery, lumber yard, fuel dealer, harness shop, shoe shop, blacksmith shop, meat market, elevator, a doctor's office, a law office, and one saloon.[46]

Some names that are familiar to Little House fans were on the first official records of the town.

"Walnut Grove was incorporated on March 18, 1879. Its name came from the beautiful grove of walnut trees along the banks of Plum Creek. The first village officials were: Elias Bedal, president; T. Quartan, J. Leo and C. Clementson, trustees; F.H. Hill, recorder; W.H. Owens (William Oleson), treasurer; J. Russell, constable; and Charles Ingalls, justice of peace."[47]

On his new farm, Charles soon built a small house out of lumber, probably not too unlike the one pictured on TV. As in the series, the Ingalls did business in Walnut Grove, went to church there, and Mary and Laura went to school there. Oddly enough, though, the name of the town is never, ever mentioned in Laura's book. Walnut Grove is only called "town," which was three miles away from their farm.

The real town of Walnut Grove in its very early days.[48]

In *Pioneer Girl*, Laura recalled her recollections of going to church in Walnut Grove.

"Walnut Grove was only a tiny town, with two small stores, a blacksmith shop, a little school house and a few houses where people lived, but the summer before they had built a church. There was Sunday school every Sunday and a sermon preached by the Home Missionary Reverend Alden."

In the Plum Creek book, Laura expanded on that. She recalled a tall, skinny man who spoke during the service. While he spoke, she looked at the butterflies, the blowing grass, the bottoms of the shingles overhead, the hair ribbons on the girls' heads, her hands, her fingers, and her fingernails. Laura thought he would never stop talking.

That man was Reverend Alden.

When the service was over, he shook Pa's hand, he shook Ma's hand, and he shook little Laura's hand. Laura liked him then, even if she had thought that he would never stop talking. He called Mary and Laura his "country girls," and they thought that was nice. Perhaps he said that to most of the little girls, but he could not have imagined that his phrase "country girls" would become the title of one of the most watched television episodes ever.

But then, he probably didn't imagine television, either.

In the Little House television show, Reverend Alden was one of the main characters, appearing throughout the series. He was a warm, caring person who faithfully served his community and was especially close to the Ingalls. He was portrayed by actor Dabbs Greer, who also had many other television credits, both as good guys and bad guys. He is most often remembered, though, as Reverend Alden, definitely a good guy. Greer passed away in 2009 at the age of ninety.

In Laura's books, Reverend Alden was also definitely a good guy, but not so prominent as in the TV show. In real life, the Ingalls soon moved on from Walnut Grove, and in the next book after Plum Creek, when the Ingalls were living by Silver Lake, Reverend Alden made a brief appearance there, in the winter of 1879-80.

"We must trust in the Lord to do all things for our best good," said

Reverend Alden. "Shall we have a short prayer meeting, all of us together, when you finish the dishes?"

"Yes, Brother Alden, I should like that," said Ma. "I am sure we all would."

... When Ma came in, Reverend Alden stood up and said they would all have the refreshment of prayer together before saying good night.

They all knelt down by their chairs, and Reverend Alden asked God, Who knew their hearts and their secret thoughts, to look down on them there, and to forgive their sins and help them to do right. A quietness was in the room while he spoke. Laura felt as if she were hot, dry, dusty grass parching in a drought, and the quietness was a cool and gentle rain falling on her. It truly was a refreshment."[49]

Laura based the Reverend Alden in her books on a real person she had known. He was a Congregationalist minister who planted the church in Walnut Grove, while he pastored another church farther east.

An article in the *New York Times* titled "Swindling at the Agencies," published August 15, 1878, said the following.

"Bismarck, Dakota Territory, Aug. 14 –

The investigation by Gen. Hammond, Indian Inspector, into the affairs of the Fort Berthold Agency, proves another agent to be a pious fraud and a cheat. The agent is Rev. E. H. Alden, formerly a Congregational minister of Minnesota, who could not support himself at his calling. He is shown to have swindled in a small way, lacking the courage to draw any large vouchers or enter any large frauds with the trader. The worst he did was to carry his wife on the pay-roll while she was in Minnesota, and to perjure himself in *swearing that she was present on the agency and actually performed the work of clerk; to draw a voucher for $50 for a carpenter, and pocket the money, and to lie to the Indians until they came to regard him as the prince of liars, and threatened to kill him if he did not leave."*[50]

Of course, that does not give the other side of the story at all, and there probably was one. Here is a letter from Alden concerning his resignation as Indian agent.

"In consequence of the many difficulties and discouragements of this position, with which I felt unable to cope longer, and the apparent fact that I could not accomplish what I most desired, I resigned the position as agent last February. My resignation was accepted in March, and I have been looking for my successor every week since. The wages of my employees being reduced by the department, some of them could not be induced to remain and their places have been partially filled by such help as could be obtained upon so much uncertainty and short notice. I have done the best I could under the circumstances, and am rather surprised that the work has moved along so smoothly and well as it has.

... Finally, I would say I came to this agency with a strong desire to help this people, and their greatest good has been my motive during my stay. When I leave them it will be with the consciousness that though my administration has not been free from mistakes, I have endeavored honestly and faithfully to do my duty. I have not been able to accomplish for these Indians the work I had hoped, but I leave it to my successor, who, I hope, may be sustained by the department and surrounded at the agency by such as shall aid him in this noble work of lifting the fallen.

Very respectfully, Your obedient servant, E. H. Alden, United States Indian Agent"[51]

In the first season of the show, in "The Voice of Tinker Jones" episode, Harriet Oleson offered to buy a bell for the new church. There was a catch to Harriet's philanthropy: the bell had to have a plaque noting her godly generosity. The church members argued over whether or not to honor Harriet in such a way. The unspoken question was: if Harriet Oleson was on the church bell, would God still come in that church?

The problem was solved when Tinker Jones, a mute artisan, with the help of the local children, constructed the bell – without Harriet's plaque – and peace returned to the congregation.

In Laura's Plum Creek book, Pa's boots helped buy the church bell. His boots were cracked and mended and then cracked again. He had three dollars to buy a badly needed pair of boots, but he gave that three dollars for the church bell. Without dramatization, Laura remembered that incident like this:

"He was going to get him some new boots because his old ones had holes in them, but when he came back there were no new boots. Ma asked him about them and he said they were trying to get money enough to buy a bell for the church and he had given Rev. Alden his boot money to help. Ma looked so sorry and said "Oh Charles!" But Pa said he could mend his old boots and they would do."[52]

In episode three of the first season, "The 100 Mile Walk," a hailstorm destroyed the Ingalls' harvest. With no money and no crop, Charles, in his ragged boots, left Walnut Grove to find work, along with other men from the town.

There is a similar incident in the Plum Creek book, where grasshoppers, not hail, destroyed the crop. Pa was counting on that wheat crop to pay for new boots, and the house he had built, and food and fuel to make it through the next winter. With no crop, they were in dire straits, so Charles walked a hundred miles east, back where the grasshoppers did not strike, to find work helping more fortunate farmers with their harvest. And Charles had to walk that hundred miles there and back in worn out boots.

Charles Ingalls, with bright blue eyes and bushy, bushy beard

Laura remembered in *Pioneer Girl* that he was too broke to pay train fare.

"There were no crops to the harvested nor anything to live on until crops could grow again and there was no money to buy food. And so one day, Pa told us all goodby, put on his hat and carrying his coat over his shoulder, started walking east to where there was harvesting to be done. He walked because there was no money to pay for a ride

on the train and he must go where he could get work in the harvest fields to earn money for us to live on through the winter."

That grasshopper plague really happened. In her unpublished memoir, Laura wrote of that astounding attack.

"The weather was just right and the crops grew and grew. At dinner one day, Pa was telling us that the wheat in our field was so tall it would just stand under his arms, with long, beautiful heads and filling nicely. He said the grain was all soft and milky yet but was so well grown he felt sure we would have a wonderful crop.

Just then we heard some one call and Mrs. Nelson was in the doorway. She was all out of breath with running, wringing her hands and almost crying. "The grasshoppers are coming! The grasshoppers are coming!" she shrieked "Come and look!"

We all ran to the door and looked around. Now and then a grasshopper dropped on the ground but we couldn't see anything to be so excited about. "Look at the sun! Yoost look at the sun!" cried Mrs. Nelson, pointing to the sky.

We raised our faces and looked straight into the sun. It had been shining brightly but now there was a light colored, fleecy cloud over its face as it did not hurt our eyes.

And then we saw that the cloud was grasshoppers, their wings a shiny white making a screen between us and the sun. They were dropping to the ground like hail in a hailstorm faster and faster. "It will ruin ta crops, alretty to eat ta wheat!" wailed Mrs. Nelson forgetting her Norwegian speech in her excitement.

Our dinner was forgotten. Mrs. Nelson ran home sobbing. Pa put on his hat and went out toward his beautiful wheat field while Ma stood in the door and watched the cloud of grasshoppers settling on the land.

Pa tried to save his wheat. He hauled straw and manure and put it in piles around and through the field, then set it on fire, hoping that the smoke might keep the grasshoppers away. He worked all the rest of the day and all night, but the grasshoppers paid no attention to the smoke. They ate through the stems of the tall wheat as well as the heads of grain so that it all fell down and was eaten and destroyed. They ate every green thing, the garden, the grass, the leaves on the trees. Our chickens ate grasshoppers until they would eat no more. The fish in the creek ate all they could hold. Everywhere we stepped we mashed grasshoppers and they crawled up under our skirts and down the backs of our necks.

The second day at noon Pa gave up fighting them. He came in the house all tired out, with his eyes all swollen and red from the smoke and lack of sleep. He told us the wheat was gone and that the grasshoppers were laying their eggs.

The day after this which was the third day since they came, the grasshoppers began to walk toward the west. Every one was walking in the same direction like an army. They did not stop nor go around anything but went straight on over or through whatever they came to. They came to the east side of the house, walked up it, over the roof and down the other side. There was an open window up stairs on the east side and those that came to the window walked on in. There were hundreds of them in the room when Ma thought of it and ran to shut the window. Pa tried with a stick to turn some of them, but they wouldn't go a step any direction except west."

Technically, they were not grasshoppers but Rocky Mountain locusts. The infestation that Laura remembered occurred in 1874 and 1875 and devastated much of the crop yield in the center of the continent. Below is a drawing of the grasshopper infestation from the 1874 Yearbook of the Missouri State Board of Agriculture, Report of the State Entomologist.

A swarm of Locusts falling upon and devouring a wheat-field.

The worst year for those locusts was 1875, known as the Year of the Locust. America has not seen an infestation like that year, either before or since.

"When the Skies Turned to Black" discussed that unique plague.

"Lush gardens and fields of a wide range of crops were reduced to a barren, desert like appearance within a matter of hours. Crops that were needed to sustain a family and their farm animals were destroyed leaving no means of support during the coming winter."

"When conditions were ideal, they could multiply into the billions, travel over long distances, and consume virtually anything and everything that was remotely edible. Their native homelands were the dry Rocky Mountain upland region of primarily Colorado, Wyoming and Montana. After hatching out in the spring of the year, the locusts would travel eastward in search of food. In years where the number of those hatched was unusually large, the food supply was stripped rather quickly driving them ever eastward in search of new food supplies. Kansas and Nebraska were usually among their first targets and were frequently the most devastated but the swarms spread over a large area stretching north from the interior of Canada and extending all the way to the south border of Texas. The eastern regions of Nebraska and Kansas along with the western regions of Minnesota, Iowa, and Missouri were the areas most devastated."[53]

The *History of Henry and St. Clair County in Missouri*, written in 1883, eight years after the grasshopper plague, said this.

"It was the year 1875 that will long be remembered by the people of at least four states, as the grasshopper year. The scourge struck Western Missouri April, 1875, and commenced devastating some of the fairest portions of our noble commonwealth. They gave Henry [County] an earnest and overwhelming visitation, and demonstrated with an amazing rapidity that their appetite was voracious, and that everything green belonged to them for their sustenance. They came in swarms, they came by the millions, they came in legions, they came by the mile, and they darkened the heavens in their flight, or blackened the earth's surface, where in myriads they sought their daily meal. Henry County was visited from about the first week of May, and remained until the 1st of June, 1875, and during that time, every spear of wheat, oats, flax and corn were eaten close to the

ground. Potatoes and all vegetables received the same treatment, and on the line of their march, ruin stared the farmer in the face, and starvation knocked loudly at his door."[54]

One eyewitness to the plague tried to measure the extent of the grasshopper swarm.

"According to the first-hand account of A. L. Child transcribed by Riley et al. (1880), a swarm of Rocky Mountain locusts passed over Plattsmouth, Nebraska, in 1875. By timing the rate of movement as the insects streamed overhead for 5 days and by telegraphing to surrounding towns, he was able to estimate that the swarm was 1,800 miles long and at least 110 miles wide."[55]

Not surprisingly, in *By the Banks of Plum Creek*, Laura tied that locust plague in with the plague that hit Egypt in Moses' time.

"And the locusts went up over the land of Egypt, and rested in all the coasts of Egypt; very grievous were they. "For they covered the face of the whole earth, so that the land was darkened; and they did eat every herb of the land, and all the fruits of the trees which the hail had left; and there remained not any green thing on the trees, or in the herbs of the field, through all the land of Egypt."[56]

Again, in the show "The 100 Mile Walk," hail, not grasshoppers, destroyed the Ingalls crop. However, Laura and Almanzo experienced a loss of a wheat crop to hail during the first years of their marriage. At the time, 1886, they were homesteading in Dakota Territory. Almanzo began to harvest the wheat, but after a couple of turns around the field, he decided it would be better if he waited a day or two. That same afternoon a hailstorm came, with balls of ice as big as eggs, and covered the ground with a pebbly layer of ice.

"Manly went out to look at the wheatfield and came in sober enough. "There is no wheat to cut," he said. "It is all threshed and pounded into the ground. Three thousand dollars worth of wheat planted, and it's the wrong time of the year."[57]

So when the show said that a crop could be destroyed by hail, they got that right, although the scriptwriters kind of combined what happened to the Ingalls and the Wilders.

In episode 21 of the first season, "Survival," the Ingalls were caught in a blizzard while traveling from Mankato back to Walnut Grove. They found shelter in a log cabin and waited out the storm there. The reality is that storms at that time were fierce and people often were caught in blizzards, at great danger to themselves. The storms were so intense that settlers had to tie a rope to the house, just to find their way back from their barns when they did chores.

Laura remembered such blizzards in *Pioneer Girl*.

"Soon it was winter again and it was a terrible winter. There was blizzard after blizzard when the wind blew the snow in such whirling fury then one could not see into it all and not tell where he was going. We learned that a dark cloud lying close to the horizon in the northwest meant that a blizzard was coming and that it moved so swiftly it would be on us soon, sometimes in only a few minutes."

... Pa fastened one end of a long rope to the corner of the house nearest the barn; the other end he fastened at the barn door. In a blizzard he would go from barn to barn with one hand on the rope to keep from getting lost. As soon as he saw the cloud in the west, he would hurry to the barn to feed the stock and make everything snug against the storm. Usually he came back to the house with his hand on the rope. People froze to death in blizzards, within a few feet of

their own houses not able to find them. One man got lost and wandered until he was tired out. Then he took shelter under the creek bank and the snow drifted over him while he went to sleep. They found him in the spring when the show went off."

In *By the Banks of Plum Creek,* Laura wrote that Pa Ingalls was caught out in such a blizzard. He was walking home from Walnut Grove, a trip of three miles. Halfway home, the blizzard caught him and he fell into a snow-covered dip on the bank of the creek. He stayed there for three days, covered with snow and huddled close to the ground. When the storm ended, he saw that all the time he was huddled and freezing, he was within sight of his house, had he been able to see it through the storm.

Laura's book *The Long Winter* talks about a whole winter that was full of blizzards. Our book *The Long, Hard Winter of 1880-81 – What Was it Really Like?* goes through the story of that incredible year of blizzards, unlike any remembered before or since. Therefore, when the *Little House on the Prairie* writers depicted the Ingalls getting stranded in a blizzard, they had a good basis for that story.

In the series, Miss Beadle was the first schoolteacher. In real life, when Walnut Grove first became a settlement, the postmaster Lafayette Bedal turned his living room into the first school and taught students there. *On the Banks of Plum Creek* tells of how Laura and Mary first met their teacher, who was not Mr. Bedal, but Miss Eva Beadle. Laura described her as well dressed and sweet, with a particularly lovely smile.

The actress who portrayed Miss Beadle was Charlotte Stewart, just as lovely and charming as the lady in Laura's book. Although she wasn't really a teacher, in 2006 she was nominated for a "Teacher of the Year" award, presented by TV Land Awards. In an interview on Prairiefans.com, Miss Stewart talked about her experience on the show.

"I absolutely loved being on the Walnut Grove set when we were shooting in Simi Valley. It really was like stepping into the old west. I felt so comfortable in the clothes and playing the part of a teacher to the children."[58]

On the Banks of Plum Creek pictured Miss Beadle as gracious. Nellie Oleson was also introduced in that book. This is how Laura saw her.

"Nellie Oleson was very pretty. Her yellow hair hung in long curls, with two big blue ribbon bows on top. Her dress was thin white lawn, with little blue flowers scattered over it, and she wore shoes."[59]

Notice the distinction there between Laura and Nellie: Nellie wore shoes.

In *Pioneer Girl*, Laura wrote of Nellie and Willie Owens.

"The ones we came to know best were the Kennedys and Nellie and Willie Owens. Mr. Owens kept one of the stores and we were sometimes allowed to go home with them and stay a little while after school. They had such wonderful toys ... beautiful but she would not let me play with them.

Nellie had the most wonderful doll that she kept wrapped up in soft paper most of the time. She would take it out and hold it up before our eyes, then wrap it up again and put it back in its box. She and Willie would help themselves to candy out of the store and eat it before us never offering us any. We would not have been allowed to be so rude and selfish but Mrs. Owen never seemed to care."

You can see that Nellie Owens became Nellie Oleson. The 1950's detective show *Dragnet* said, "*Ladies and gentlemen: the story you are about to hear is true. Only the names have been changed to protect the innocent.*" In Nellie's case, her name was changed from Owens to Oleson to protect the guilty.

In the seventh show of the first season, "Town Party, Country Party," the Olesons had a party at their house. In return, the Ingalls had a party out by Plum Creek. Laura knew that a crab hid under a certain rock. She managed to get Nellie to go to that spot, the crab scared Nellie, who then fell into the creek, and everyone was very delighted.

Except for Nellie.

In real life, Laura recalled the crab and Nellie and the leaches in her unpublished account of the same incident.

"When we were playing by ourselves we didn't wade in that pool, for we didn't like the bloodsuckers they seemed such nasty things. But when the girls from town came out, as they often did to play with us, we would lead them by the old crab's stone and when he would chase them they would run screaming on into the bloodsucker's pool.

When they came out on the bank and saw the little, long flat bloodsuckers stuck on their feet and legs, they would try to brush them off. When they found they couldn't they would dance around and kick and scream while I would roll on the grass and laugh until Mary would make me come and help her pull them off. They would come again but they never caught us at our little trick of leading them into the pool on purpose and they never learned that the old crab lived under the stone and that the pool was the home of the bloodsuckers.

Mary was tender hearted and sometimes said we ought not to frighten our company so, but I said, when we went to town to see them they wouldn't let us handle their toys, the wonderful doll that would open and shut its eyes we were not allowed to hold and we could only look at their other things while they showed them to us; so I just would play my way when they came to see us. Finally Ma said we must not do so anymore, but Pa's blue eyes twinkled when he heard about it."

That story was included with even greater detail in *On the Banks of Plum Creek*. It might be called the story of two crabs – the one under the rock and Nellie.

In the "Country Girls" episode, Charles and Caroline talked about how Laura loved her first experience at school.

"Charles: It's hard to believe that's the same little girl we could hardly get out of bed this morning.

Caroline: I hoped she'd like it. I wasn't sure.

Charles: Oh, she'll be fine. She sure was feisty about that Nellie Oleson.

Caroline: I wonder why.

Charles: You haven't met her mother."

Just as in the show, Nellie Oleson was a prominent character in Laura's books. She was, in fact, the main antagonist. The books did not emphasize Nellie's parents.

In the television series, on the other hand, Nellie was the main antagonist, but, quite honestly, her mother was also pretty antagonizing. They formed kind of an antag team.

When the show included Nellie Oleson as noxious Nellie, they cast well. She was portrayed by Alison Arngrim, who did a tremendous job, even though the long blonde rolls were just a wig. Alison first tried out for the role of Laura. Then she tried for the role of Mary, Laura's gentle sister. The producers did not give her either of those roles, but instead put her in the role of Nellie.

Give credit where credit is due – they done good!

Arngrim was a Young Artist Award–Former Child Star "Lifetime Achievement" Award honoree, for her distinctive work as Nellie on *Little House on the Prairie*. It seems like almost everybody knows who Nellie Oleson is! Of all the actors and actresses on that show, the one who leaves the strongest impression is probably Alison Arngrim for her Nellie Oleson role. Her battles with Melissa Gilbert's Laura are television classics.

But isn't life strange? It turns out that Alison and Melissa were very good friends and after the show closed, remained in contact with each other through the ensuring decades. And every time they have a serious disagreement, Alison doesn't cuss or fuss at Melissa – she just mutters, *"Country girl!"*

About halfway through the first season appeared a two-hour special entitled "The Lord is My Shepherd." Of course, that is from the most famous Psalm in the Bible, the 23rd Psalm.

> The LORD is my shepherd; I shall not want.
> He maketh me to lie down in green pastures:
> he leadeth me beside the still waters.
> He restoreth my soul: he leadeth me in the paths of
> righteousness for his name's sake.

Yea, though I walk through
the valley of the shadow of death,
I will fear no evil:
for thou art with me;
thy rod and thy staff they comfort me.
Thou preparest a table before me
in the presence of mine enemies:
thou anointest my head with oil;
my cup runneth over.
Surely goodness and mercy shall follow me
all the days of my life:
and I will dwell in the house of the LORD for ever.

When this show aired, most people were familiar with that Psalm. Not so today. Three very bright young college students were contestants on the quiz show *Jeopardy* and none of them could finish this phrase, "The Lord is my _____."

Laura could. In our book *Big Bible Lessons from Laura Ingalls' Little Books*, we talked about Laura's love for that Psalm.

"In The Long Winter, Laura wrote about the teacher beginning the school day by reading the 23rd Psalm to the class. Laura mentioned that she knew all the Psalms by heart, of course. But there are 150 Psalms, all of which she knew by heart – of course! Even though she knew them all, she loved hearing the 23rd, from "The Lord is my shepherd: I shall not want,' " to "Surely goodness and mercy shall follow me all the days of my life: and I will dwell in the house of the Lord forever."

After that, the Bible was closed and the schoolbooks were opened.

That was a typical American school, starting the school day with the most important subject – God, the Bible, and prayer."

So then, with such a title and being a two-hour production, you know "The Lord is My Shepherd" episode has special meaning.

In that show, Charles and Caroline had a new baby boy, Charles Frederick Ingalls. The show depicted Laura as being jealous of the new arrival. The little boy died soon afterward, and Laura felt very guilty. The show ended with Laura realizing how much she meant to her Pa.

In real life, after the grasshoppers ate the wheat, and after Pa had returned from working a hundred miles east of Walnut Grove, Laura remembered this.

"We went to town, that winter, to live in a little house behind the church, and not far from the schoolhouse, so that Mary and I could go to school. Coming home from school one day, we found a strange woman getting supper and a little brother beside ma on the bed. We were very proud of him and always hurried home from school to see him."[60]

That was November 1, 1875, and the little boy's name was Charles Frederick Ingalls, exactly as the show had it. The show where Freddy was born ran on December 18, 1974, in the hundredth year after the actual occurrence. Of course, Laura was not really jealous of her little brother at all but rejoiced in having him, as did the whole family. After three girls, the Ingalls family was quite grateful to have a little boy.

But Charles lost a second crop to grasshoppers that had

hatched out from the previous summer's infestation, and then he became disgusted with Walnut Grove.

When the *Little House on the Prairie* series changed over to *Little House – A New Beginning* in season nine, the show had the Ingalls move to Burr Oak, Iowa. That effectively took them out of the series, leaving Laura and Almanzo Wilder as the focus. In real life, after Pa's disgust with the grasshoppers, the Ingalls left Walnut Grove and headed for Burr Oak, Iowa in the fall of 1876. Ma and Pa were going to help a friend run a small hotel in Burr Oak. Laura did not include their time in Burr Oak in any of her books.

On the way to Iowa, the Ingalls stopped to stay for a while with the family of Peter Ingalls, Pa's brother, in Minnesota. While they were there, this happened.

"Little Brother was not well and the Dr. came. I thought that would cure him as it had Ma when the Dr. came to see her. But Little Brother got worse instead of better and one awful day he straightened out his little body and was dead."[61]

That's all Laura wrote about such a sad event. That awful day was August 27, 1876. Pa's only son, named after him as Charles Frederick Ingalls, was only nine months old when he died. He never made it to his first birthday. Little Freddy was buried on Peter Ingalls' farm and the site of the grave is unknown today.

The show was basically right about Freddy, but in reality, the little boy's death was worse than in the show.

Pa was always trying to run a farm to feed the family, and he only had girls to help him. Ma did not believe that girls should work outside like men, so usually they didn't. That left all the farm work on Pa's shoulders. Most men had sons to help them grow the crops, while the women took care of the gardens and many domestic chores. However, Charles had no sons to help him. His only little boy died, and he had no more sons, either born or adopted. It is said that Pa most regretted not getting to play the fiddle for his son, and that even many years afterward, Ma talked about how things would have been different on the farm if little Freddy had lived.[62]

In the episode "A Most Precious Gift," Caroline Ingalls became pregnant again. That was Pa's chance to have another son. Caroline was afraid that Charles would be disappointed if the baby was a girl. When the new baby Grace was born, Charles loved her just as much as he loved his other three girls.

In real life, after their stopover to stay with relatives in Minnesota, and after Freddy's death, the Ingalls continued on to Burr Oak, Iowa, where Charles and Caroline helped run the hotel. Burr Oak today is a village of less than 200 people, located just south of the Minnesota border.

"We felt so badly to go on and leave Freddy," Laura remembered, *"but in a little while we had to go on to Iowa to help keep the hotel. It was a cold miserable little journey and we were glad when we drove into Burr Oak and got out of the wagon into the warmth and comfort of the house."*[63]

Their work with the hotel did not work out, Pa did other work there and they moved out of the hotel into a house. Laura recalled that while they were living in that house, she came home one day and found this.

"I helped Ma with the work, ran errands and every day worked sums on multiplication; looking back at the multiplication table to help me when I couldn't remember. One day when I came back from an errand that had taken me a long time, I found a new little sister. Her name was Grace. Her hair was golden like Mary's and her eyes were blue and bright like Pa's."[64]

Grace Pearl Ingalls was born May 23, 1877 in Burr Oak, Iowa. She was the last of Caroline and Charles' children. No more were born and they never adopted any. Their family was a quartet of girls, Mary, Laura, Carrie and Grace.

Grace was ten years younger than Laura, so she did not play a big role in Laura's books, as Mary and Carrie did. When Grace was grown, she became a teacher. In 1901, she married Nate Dow. Grace was 24 and he was 42. They never had children and lived their whole lives either in or near De Smet.

Grace Ingalls as a young lady.

In the television series, Grace Ingalls was played by another set of identical twins, Brenda and Wendi Turnbaugh.

"Between 1978 and 1982 Brenda and Wendi shared the part of Grace Ingalls on Little House on the Prairie. Grace is the youngest member of the Ingalls family, born in the episode "A Most Precious Gift". But Wendi and Brenda didn't start playing the part until a couple of episodes later - in an episode called "As Long As We're Together".

After the success with the Greenbush Twins (who shared the part of Grace's older sister Carrie between 1974 and 1982), the producers of "Little House" were determined to find twins for the part of little Grace as well. Kent McCray (producer of "Little House on the Prairie") was a close friend to Wendi & Brenda's grandmother. He told her he needed twins to play Grace, and was thrilled when she told him her daughter had just given birth to twins!

Wendi & Brenda got the part of Grace, and kept it until the entire Ingalls family (except the second-oldest daughter Laura) left Walnut Grove (and the show) in 1982."[65]

Working with twins helped the show's producers follow child labor laws, because each little girl only had to work half the time, if acting can be called work. So *Little House on the Prairie* had two sets of identical twins, one set acting as Carrie and the other set acting as Grace.

Again, the name of the episode where Grace was born was "A Most Precious Gift," and, in real life, surely Charles viewed her that way, as did Caroline, Mary, Laura and Carrie, even if she wasn't a little boy.

Perhaps the most memorable episode in the history of *Little*

House on the Prairie was *"I'll Be Waving as You Drive Away."* TV Guide named it as one of TV's Top 100 Episodes of all time.[66] It was very sad. It was also based on truth.

The series had included a subtheme of Mary's eyesight weakening and she began to wear glasses. In the next to last show of season four, Mary's eyesight worsened. A doctor told Charles that her eyesight could not be saved and she would soon be blind. Pa did not tell Mary that until, in fact, she was almost totally blind. In the show, Mary's reaction to her affliction was one of horror and bitterness.

In the second episode of that two-parter, Mary went to a school for the blind in Iowa. There she met Adam Kendall, who eventually became her husband. As she left the school to go back to Walnut Grove, he told her, "I'll be waving as you drive away." Of course, she couldn't see him wave, and that line was the title of the show.

In real life, the Ingalls family moved from Burr Oak, Iowa back to Walnut Grove, Minnesota in 1878. They bought a plot of land and built a house there. Pa worked at whatever jobs he could find. Then, in 1879 –

"Mary was taken suddenly sick with a pain in her head and grew worse quickly. She was delirious with an awful fever and Ma cut off her long, beautiful hair to keep her head cooler.

We feared for several days that she would not get well and one morning when I looked at her I saw one side of her face drawn out of shape. Ma said Mary had had a stroke and as I looked at her I remembered her oak tree away back in Wisconsin that had been struck by lightening all down one side.

After the stroke Mary began to get better, but she could not see well. Pa had Dr. Welcome come to help Dr. Hoyt with them but he said the nerves of her eyes had the worst of the stroke and were dying, that nothing could be done. They had a long name for her sickness and said it was the results of the measels [sic] from which she had never wholly recovered.

As Mary grew stronger her eyes grew weaker until when she could sit up in the big chair among the pillows, she could hardly see at all. The last thing Mary saw was the bright, blue of Grace's eyes as Grace stood holding by her chair, looking up at her."[67]

Mary Ingalls as a young lady, her unseeing eyes not looking directly at the camera.[68]

When Laura wrote of Mary's affliction in her books, she said very little. The show's scriptwriters made Mary's illness a big production, but Laura described it in only a few words. For the scriptwriters, it was a show. For Laura, it was a real memory, treated very briefly at the beginning of *By the Shores of Silver Lake*.

"Mary and Carrie and baby Grace and Ma had all had scarlet fever... Far worst of all, the fever had settled in Mary's eyes, and Mary was blind.

She was able to sit up now, wrapped in quilts in Ma's old hickory rocking chair. All that long time, week after week, when she could still see a little, but less every day, she had never cried. Now she could not see even the brightest light any more. She was still patient and brave.

Her beautiful golden hair was gone. Pa had shaved it close because of the fever, and her poor shorn head looked like a boy's. Her blue eyes were still beautiful, but they did not know what was before them, and Mary herself could never look through them again to tell Laura what she was thinking without saying a word."[69]

That was it. Not a two-part episode, just three short paragraphs. Laura did not really cover Mary's going blind in her books. She only referred back to it as having already happened between books.

"I'll Be Waving as You Drive Away" was true in its basic premise. Mary did go blind. The scriptwriters then varied from the details of Mary's real life.

Mary Ingalls did, in fact, attend a school for the blind in Iowa. Laura taught school in Dakota to help pay for Mary's education to learn how to function better without sight. Mary enrolled in the Blind Asylum in Vinton, Iowa on November

23, 1881, two years after losing her sight. She graduated from that institution on June 12, 1889.

Again real life was a bit more stark than the TV story. Mary did not meet an Adam Kendall who became her husband. She never married. She did not herself start a school for the blind. She lived the rest of her life with Caroline and Charles, then at their passing with Grace or Carrie. After Charles died in 1902, Mary and Ma were hard pressed for income to live on. Ma rented out the upstairs room of their house in De Smet and Mary, although blind, wove and sold fly nets, open weave blankets for horses. She also played organ for the church in De Smet and wrote articles for church periodicals. She lived four years after Caroline died, passing away on October 17, 1928, at sixty-three years of age.

In real life, Mary was never bitter about her blindness or not being married and raising a family. She was a happy, fulfilled woman, filled with her faith in God.

In one of the ironies of life, Mary's blindness turned out to be a blessing for all of us, as we discussed in our book *Big Bible Lessons from Laura's Little Books*.

"One of the great adversities that the Ingalls faced was Mary's blindness. Laura and Mary were very close. They were sister best friends. Laura's books often include the walks she and Mary took, when they enjoyed being out on the prairie and with each other. After her beloved sister Mary lost her sight, Laura showed her love not just by what she felt, but by what she did.

In By the Shores of Silver Lake, when Ma and the four girls took a train west to meet Pa, they went into a hotel in Tracy, Minnesota. Ma walked in first, carrying Grace, the youngest. Then Carrie walked closely behind Ma. Finally came Laura, leading Mary. They ate dinner in the hotel. It cost twenty-five cents, and they could eat all they wanted. Laura cut up Mary's meat and buttered her bread. Mary had not been blind long, but already she had learned to use a fork without seeing and could feed herself.

On that train ride, and for years afterward, Laura was Mary's eyes.

"A thin man with bristly eyebrows and long mustaches and an Adam's apple just went by. He can't walk straight, the train's going so fast. I wonder what – Oh, Mary! He's turning a little handle on the wall at the end of the car, and water's coming out!

The water's pouring right into a tin cup. Now he's drinking it. His Adam's apple bobs. He's filling the cup again. He just turns the handle and the water comes right out. How do you suppose it – Mary! He's set that cup on a little shelf. Now he's coming back."

Laura took the time to help Mary see. Her giving came back to her when word pictures, as she painted for Mary, filled Laura's books."

We were blessed because in helping Mary, Laura learned how to describe wonderfully the things she saw around her.

Melissa Sue Anderson played Mary Ingalls on the show. She actually seems like kind, gentle Mary. She received an Emmy nomination for "I'll Be Waving As You Drive Away," a high honor for her efforts.

Furthermore, it seems that the producers went the extra mile in some of their casting, because Melissa Anderson bears some resemblance to the character of the character she played. The TV information site says, *"Many actresses are not like the characters they play, but Melissa Sue Anderson wasn't one of them.*

Melissa was born September 26, 1962, in Berkeley, California. In real life, she was very much the same as Mary Ingalls--a quiet, slightly shy girl who would rather read a book than climb a tree."[70]

Wikia.com's Little House collection says this about Melissa. "She has been described as mild mannered and unpretentious, similar to her Mary Ingalls character...Once she dated Frank Sinatra, Jr., who at the time was more than twice her age. She says, "It was fun, but never really wild. That's just not me."

The three young ladies who played Laura, Mary and Nellie each wrote books about their Little House years. Melissa Anderson's book was titled *The Way I See It*. And how did she see it? Very delicately, thank you. Actually, the publishers wanted more of an exposé on the wild goings on in Little House land. But Melissa Anderson only said nice things. *"My editor wanted me to be completely honest,"* she observed. *"I tend to be nice. They said it doesn't have to be so nice."*[71] Many reviewers don't appreciate her book for just that reason. Nobody is slammed, nobody is slimed, and nothing slummy is revealed. She actually discusses the shows instead of the extracurricular activities.

In an interview, Miss Anderson explained why she didn't write much about Melissa Gilbert, who played Laura. *"I honestly do not have a lot of memories of the two of us,"* she said in an interview this afternoon. *"We were very, very different."*[72] Just as the real Laura and Mary were quite different, so the two young ladies who played them were also quite dissimilar.

The special production about Mary going blind was intended to be the very last episode of *Little House on the Prairie*. However, that show attracted more viewers than any other in the series, and NBC made the decision to continue the series.[73]

In real life, of course, Mary received no award. Shortly after she was struck with her blindness, the Ingalls moved away from Walnut Grove forever. That was the end of their life in *On the Banks of Plum Creek*, and the story continued in the next book and at another town.

Chapter 7

Silver Lake in Dakota

By this time, you might be getting the impression that the real Charles Ingalls was a rolling stone. He and his family lived in Wisconsin, Kansas, Wisconsin again, Minnesota, then Iowa, then Minnesota again. Pa certainly gathered no moss, although he did have a beard.

The fourth season of the television series was its most popular, ending with the story of Mary losing her sight. At the start of the fifth season, the Ingalls and others left Walnut Grove, Minnesota and moved to Winoka, Dakota Territory. Mary had moved there to teach in a school for the blind, so the family followed.

Exactly where is Winoka?

We don't know where Winoka is, because Winoka is nowhere. Unlike other towns in the series that were taken from Laura's books, Winoka is a fictitious town. Of course, Dakota Territory was real, and eventually became the states of North Dakota and South Dakota. The populations of both states are small, and it is a bit surprising that some small hamlet there has not changed its name to Winoka.

But none has, so there is no Winoka. Funny how the writers

came up with a name that just sounds like it really ought to exist somewhere.

In 1879, not long after Mary had lost her vision, the Ingalls family did move to Dakota Territory. Laura's fifth book, *By the Shores of Silver Lake*, begins with that move. In that book, something else happened before they left Plum Creek.

One evening Laura's dog Jack circled his bed three times and then lay down, and looked up at Laura. The next morning Jack lay dead, there where he had circled three times and peacefully spent his last night.

In the first show of the fourth season of the TV series, Laura was flustered with old Jack because she couldn't get the foxtails out of his ears. Later she came home to find him dead.

In real life, there was a real Jack, and he was really Laura's buddy. When they were traveling from Wisconsin to Kansas, this is how Laura remembered Jack.

"There was a long, scared sound off in the night and Pa said it was a wolf howling. It frightened me a little, but we were safe in the wagon with its nice tight cover to keep out the wind and the rain. The wagon was home, we had lived in it so long and Pa's rifle was hanging at the side where he could get it quickly to shoot the wolf. He wouldn't let wolves nor anything hurt us and Jack the brindle bulldog was lying under the wagon guarding us too and so we fell asleep.

Pa built a house of logs from the trees in the nearby creek bottom and when we moved into it there was only a hole in the wall where the window was to be and a quilt hung over the doorway to keep the weather out. At night Jack always lay across the doorway inside and when I was waked by the wolves howling, I would hear Jack growling and Pa would say, "Go back to sleep; Jack won't let them in." One night Pa picked me up and out of bed and carried me to the window so I could see the wolves. There were so many of them all sitting in a ring around the house, with their noses pointed up at the big, bright moon, howling as loud and long as they could, while Jack paced before the door and growled."[74]

Actually, though, Jack did not stay with Laura until he died of old age. Instead, he went with the horses when Pa made a trade on that trip.

"Pa traded the horses Pet and Parry for some larger horses and because Jack wanted to stay with Pet and Patty as he always did Pa gave him to the man who had them."[75]

When the Ingalls moved to Dakota Territory, they moved to De Smet, not Winoka. De Smet is a small town one county west of the Minnesota border and the Ingalls were some of the first settlers to live in the area. The railroad came through there in the summer of 1879; that summer Charles worked for the railroad as a clerk. The Ingalls spent the next winter in a surveyors' house owned by the railroad, and early the next year Pa filed on a homestead nearby. He also bought a lot and built a store building in the new little town.

In the TV show, the Ingalls did not like Winoka, and wound up moving back to Walnut Grove. In real life, the Ingalls did like the little town of De Smet, except possibly for some of the winters, and Charles and Caroline remained there. They homesteaded a 160-acre farm near town. After proving up and getting their 'free' farm from the government, they sold it and moved into town where Pa built a good-sized house. Today De Smet is about one square mile in size and about a thousand people live there. The building that the Ingalls lived in their first winter there still stands, as does a house that Charles built on Third Street.

Probably the biggest point of conflict between Caroline and Charles, perhaps the only real conflict, was the fact that Pa always wanted to move somewhere else other than where he was. He had his own farm in Wisconsin, close to family and friends, but he didn't like the trees and wanted to farm on the open prairie. He built a log house on the Kansas prairie and began a homestead there, only to leave a short while before the area was officially opened to homesteading. With his head start and a bit more persistence, he could have had a quarter section of good land in a mild climate, just a little north of Oklahoma. After that, he took back his Wisconsin farm from a buyer who gave up on it, then left that for the greener pastures of Minnesota. He endured a couple years of grasshopper plagues there, and left to be a partner in a hotel in Iowa, but that deal turned sour. Back in Minnesota, things were still tough, so he jumped at the chance to work for the railroad for a few months and stake out a claim for a homestead in Dakota.

That was Pa.

That was not Ma. She never liked moving. She was a homebody and wanted a settled, stable life.

At De Smet, Ma finally won that discussion. They stayed put.

In spite of that difference over moving, Caroline and Charles were a very close couple. They were geographically challenged, but their love was rock solid.

Our book *Big Bible Lessons from Laura Ingalls' Little Books* talked about the lifelong marriage of Caroline and Charles.

"In the big woods of Wisconsin, settling on the Kansas prairie with their new log cabin, in a dugout on the banks of Plum Creek, snug in the surveyors' house on the shores of Silver Lake, buried in snow during the long winter, on the homestead during Laura's golden years, and then during the rest of their lives in the house on Third Street in De Smet –

Ma and Pa Ingalls were one man, one woman, married for life. For each there was no other. Wherever their little houses were located, those little houses were all filled with their love. Ma and Pa were always there, always together, always in love. Their girls never ever had a thought that such would not be so."[76]

In a second season episode of the show, titled "For My Lady," Charles wanted to buy Caroline a new set of China. To earn the money he secretly took a carpentry job working for a pretty young widow. Harriet Oleson – who else? – suggested to Mary that Pa was working on more than the woodwork. Mary and Laura became afraid that Pa was interested in the pretty widow, and concocted plans to win him back for Ma. All was cleared up at the end when Charles presented Caroline with the new china he had worked for, a gift of his love.

The reverse situation happened in a later episode, "The Handyman." Caroline desired a bigger kitchen in which to do all her work for the family, so Charles decided to build the house bigger. However, he had to leave for work, so Caroline hired a handsome young handyman to do the job. He lived with the family while Charles was away, and again it was gentle Mary who became suspicious. Harriet Oleson again reinforced those suspicions, aided and abetted by Nellie. Mary eventually learned that she was wrong, and finally Charles returned home and finished the kitchen for his Caroline.

"I Remember, I Remember" was a warm and moving show from the popular fourth season. A flashback showed Charles and Caroline's youth, and how they got to know one another as teens. In real life, Caroline Quiner married Charles Ingalls on February 1, 1860. She was twenty and he was twenty-four. The Ingalls and the Quiners were neighbors, and three Quiners married three Ingalls, making for a lot of double first cousins.

By the Shores of Silver Lake describes the first winter that the Ingalls spent in Dakota. There is little in common between the book and the time in the show that the Ingalls lived in Winoka. In both cases, on the show and in real life, when they went to Dakota they were getting adjusted to Mary's being blind.

In the second show with the Ingalls in Winoka, titled "As Long As We're Together," Charles sold his fiddle to get enough money to buy Mary a birthday present. Caroline saw the fiddle in the window of a shop and bought it back. On Mary's birthday, Mary said that the best present she could have was to hear Pa play his fiddle. She got that present. When it was time for her to make a wish and blow out the candles, blind Mary simply said, *"I have nothing to wish for! I have everything in the world right here in this room!"*

That type of selfless love and contentment fills both the show and the books.

In the Silver Lake book, Laura does not focus greatly on

Mary's blindness, except in two ways. First, Mary was brave and never complained about her situation. Second, since Mary was blind, Laura became Mary's eyes. Pa asked Laura to do that, and it turned out that Laura was very good at it.

That winter by Silver Lake, their first winter in Dakota, was not a time of particular hardship. The winter was cold but rather normal. The house where they lived was warm and the pantry well stocked by the railroad. No great illness or plague besieged them, but it surely was a time of emotional recovery. They had lost their only son, and their eldest daughter was blind. On those long winter nights, out on the prairie by themselves, snug and warm and cozy, Ma and Pa, and Laura, Carrie, Grace and Mary spent a lot of time just being with each other. Pa played the fiddle, the firelight flickered, and love flowed in the Ingalls family. They all would have agreed with Mary in "As Long As We're Together" – *"I have everything in the world right here in this room!"*

Chapter 8

The Hard Winter

Even if you've never read it, I bet you can guess what Laura's sixth book, titled *The Long Winter*, was about.

That's right. The long winter!

In our book *The Long, Hard Winter of 1880-81 – What was it Really Like?* we talked about all the different names for it: hard winter, snow winter, black winter, and Laura called it long winter. You can tell by all those names that it was a rough winter.

"When you wonder if the winter of 1880-81 was as bad as Laura Ingalls Wilder wrote in her book The Long Winter, *remember this –*

that was the year the word "blizzard" came into common use.

Laura Ingalls Wilder wrote nine Little House books, from which the famous television program Little House on the Prairie *was taken. The sixth book in that series was* The Long Winter, *a tale of nonstop blizzards on the prairies of Dakota Territory in the winter of 1880-81.*

And during that winter, "blizzard" blew its way into the English language ...

Why did the word blizzard blow itself into the English language that year? Because more than any year in recent history, the winter of 1880-81 was the year of blizzards."[77]

The Long Winter was perhaps Laura's most involved and compelling book. She wrote in dramatic style her personal memories of that ferocious year. The Ingalls moved from their homestead into the town of De Smet for the winter, living in a store building that Pa had built. Blizzards continued from October into April, and the new little town ran out of food and fuel, making for a bleak winter, for sure, but a very riveting story.

Since the television series stayed centered on Walnut Grove, there is little in common between the show and *The Long Winter*. However, there were some features in the series that tie in with it.

In a third season episode titled "Blizzard," the schoolchildren of Walnut Grove were caught in a blizzard on their way home from school. The men of the town set out to find them.

At first, that might sound like a farfetched story, but think again. In our book about 1880-81, we cited some real life examples of just such incidents.

"That same year [1880] another teacher in Minnesota chose to stay with the children in a school during a blizzard, instead of trying to get home through the storm. George H. Wallace, a writer for the Waukesha Freeman newspaper in Waukesha, Wisconsin, wrote an account of the Winter of the Big Snow in 1933. More than fifty years later, he recalled one of the more grim memories of that memorable year.

"A school teacher in a sparsely settled district of Minnesota, where scholars came as far as six miles to attend school, was frozen to death with her scholars whom she vainly endeavored to save, when their scant fuel supply was exhausted during a 40 below zero blizzard."

Seven years after the hard winter, the winter of 1888 had two of the worst blizzards ever known. One was called the School Children's Blizzard or the Schoolhouse Blizzard.

In an article about the School Children's Blizzard of 1888, an Iroquois, South Dakota historical account describes the conditions at that time. Iroquois is a town only about fifteen miles west of De Smet.

"In 1888, pioneer children were mainly educated in one-room school houses. School houses were not only located in the small Dakota towns, but were also scattered throughout the countryside.

There were very few teachers in this new territory, so teachers of that time were mostly teenaged girls. These young girls could write their exam and earn their teacher's certificate by age 16. Most schools had one coal burning stove placed in the center of the room. There were no buses or cars. Children walked to school, or if they were lucky, rode a horse. Their walk to school may have been a mile or more. When blizzards came up, the young teacher had to decide if she should take the chance of keeping her students in the school and possibly run out of fuel and freeze or flee into the storm, hoping to find the shelter of the closest home.

Ray H. Miller's father was an early pioneer in Beadle County in 1882. His family of eight had a small but comfortable house on their homestead.

On January 12, 1888, the day started like any other. Large snow-

flakes were falling to the ground, and a slight breeze was blowing from the southwest. The morning temperatures were mild.

While watering his team of oxen, Miller's father saw a dark cloud quickly approaching from the west. The oxen, acting very uneasy, sensed something was wrong and ran to the barn.

The four oldest Miller children were in school when the storm hit. Their father started out to look for them. After walking a short distance, his face was a mask of snow and ice, and he was unable to continue. The temperature had dropped to 34 below zero and the wind was fiercely blowing at 70 miles per hour.

Mr. Miller turned around and crawled back to his house.

The school house was located near the Sprague homestead and Mr. Sprague was able to lead the students through the storm to shelter.

Many people and livestock in Dakota Territory died in this storm. Ray Miller's mother called that day a nightmare. She could not forget it, or the fact that so many people died in the storm, some found only a few feet from their homes."

... The Encyclopedia Britannica, 1893 edition, published only five years after the 1888 event, gives this account.

"In one [blizzard] which visited Dakota and the States of Montana, Minnesota, Nebraska, Kansas and Texas in January, 1888, the mercury fell within twenty-four hours from 74° above zero to 28° below in some places, and in Dakota went down to 40° below zero. In fine clear weather, with little or no warning, the sky darkened and the air was filled with snow, or ice-dust, as fine as flour, driven before a wind so furious and roaring that men's voices were inaudible at a distance of six feet. Men in the fields and children on their way from school died ere they could reach shelter; some of them having been not frozen, but suffocated from the impossibility of breathing the blizzard. Some 235 persons lost their lives. This was the worst storm since 1864; the Colorado River in Texas was frozen with ice a foot thick, for the first time in the memory of man."[78]

As you can see, at that time, schoolchildren getting caught in a blizzard was a real danger. And in fact, that did happen to Laura, as she recalled in *Pioneer Girl*.

"A widow named Garland, with two grown daughters, Florence and Lena and a son about my age named Edward but called Cap, had built a boarding house on the street back of us. Florence was hired to teach the school which began the first November and Carrie and I started to school again.

There were only fifteen pupils all strangers to each other, but beginning to feel acquainted when one still, sunny day as we were sitting quietly, studying, when the school house cracked and shook from a blow of the wind that struck the northwest corner like a mighty sledge. The sun was blotted out and all we could see from the windows was a white blur for all outside was a whirling chaos of snow.

Miss Garland looked frightened and said we would all go home: for us to put our wraps on quickly and fasten them good, that we must all stay close together and go with her. Just as we were ready to start a man named Holms came from town to help us get safely through the storm, for the schoolhouse was three blocks west of the business street and there were no houses nor anything but bare prairie between.

We started all alone together following Mr. Holms and Miss Garland, but after a few minutes Cap Garland left the others and went farther to the south. We shouted at him but he disappeared in the storm running. We were blinded by the snow, buffeted by the wind until we could hardly keep our feet[,] and awfully cold. It seemed to me that we had already gone too far and still there was no sign of buildings when suddenly we ran against the back of a building that stood at the very end of the street, the last building in town on the north. We didn't see it until we bumped against it and if we had gone just a few feet farther north we should have missed it and been out on the open prairie lost in the blizzard.

Cap Garland went straight, told the men down town that we had gone wrong and a crowd was just starting after us when we came walking up the street beside the buildings."[79]

Laura also included that memory in *The Long Winter*, written in a more dramatic fashion, and the "Blizzard" episode of the show was related to that.

The television series often focused on the Ingalls' faith, and during the hard winter of 1880-81, their Christian faith helped them through that very tough time. We talked about that near the end of our book about *The Long, Hard Winter of 1880-81*.

"Pa played the fiddle for them that winter, with a warmth that came from the spirit and not from the hay in the stove. At night, the Ingalls marched upstairs into the unheated bedrooms to the beat of his fiddle jigs, the heat of the music carrying them step by step. Every day they said their prayers, when it seemed they weren't being answered, even though sometimes they got under the covers first. And during the lowest times, they sang the highest songs.

Jesus is a Rock

Jesus is a rock in a weary land,
A weary land, a weary land,
Jesus is a rock in a weary land,
A shelter in the time of storm."

The Evergreen Shore

Then let the hurricane roar!
It will the sooner be o'er.
We'll weather the blast
And land at last
On Canaan's happy shore!"

When they all sang together of a shelter in the time of storm, singing loud enough to drown out a blizzard, don't you know that they really, really meant it."[80]

So the television series had a story about Laura and the school kids getting caught in a blizzard, and that actually happened. The series pictured the Ingalls as having a Christian faith, and they actually did. In the book *The Long Winter*, just as in the show, the children survived the blizzard; and as often portrayed in the series, the Ingalls' Christian faith helped them through their trials, including trying to stay alive during the long, hard, snow, black winter.

Chapter 9

Growing Up in the Prairie Town

What town did Laura grow up in?

Not Walnut Grove, Minnesota, but De Smet, in what became South Dakota.

Actually, De Smet is only 111 miles west of Walnut Grove, and on the same railroad line. Laura's sixth book, *Little Town on the Prairie*, tells of her growing up in De Smet.

The time setting was the year after the long, hard winter of 1880-81. That spring, the Ingalls moved back out in the country to their homestead claim near De Smet. They immediately faced a problem. They didn't have a cat – plenty of mice but no cat.

One night a mouse gnawed a hole in Pa's hair. That's right – Mickey cut off a chunk of Pa's coiffure, presumably to use in a nest. Charles had to go to a meeting of the county commissioners, because he was one, with a very unsightly bald spot in an otherwise very hairy head. Caroline became somewhat upset when he threatened to tell the other gentlemen that was how his wife cut his hair. *"Charles, you wouldn't!"* Ma exclaimed, before she saw that he was teasing her."[81]

They were soon able to buy a kitty, for the exorbitant price of fifty cents, half a day's work, and the kitty and Pa's hair grew at the same time.

There were at least a couple of notable tie-ins between *Little Town on the Prairie* and the television series.

In the "Centennial" episode, in 1876 Walnut Grove prepared to celebrate the centennial of the birth of the nation. However, when taxes went up, the oppressed citizens threatened to cancel the Fourth of July celebration. After all, a penny tax on tea helped get the whole revolution started, anyway.

Mr. Hanson even predicted that "some day a man will be taxed on what he earns!"[82]

However, a new Russian immigrant, who had lost his property because he was unable to pay his taxes, gave a heartfelt talk about what a privilege it was to live in America. The town then went ahead with its Centennial Independence Day observance, even with the higher taxes, and sure enough, eventually Americans were taxed on what they earn.

The eighth chapter of *Little Town on the Prairie*, titled "Fourth of July," tells of an Independence Day celebration in De Smet. The new little town was not organized enough to have a very big event, but they did have a spirit of independence.

Pa asked Caroline if she wanted to go to the celebration. When he told her that it included horseracing, Caroline chose not to attend, because ladies weren't real keen on horseracing. Baby Grace and Mary stayed home with her.

Charles, Laura and Carrie walked into De Smet for the Fourth of July. In town, they had a rare treat – lemonade. They did not have Dixie cups, or Yankee cups, either. They all – *the whole town* – drank out of the same bucket of lemonade, from the same dipper.

Soon a gentleman read the Declaration of Independence aloud before the crowd. When that ended, all was quiet and no one quite knew what to do. So Charles started singing and everyone joined in.

>My country 'tis of thee,
>Sweet land of liberty,
>Of thee I sing.
>Long may out land be bright
>With freedom's holy light.
>Protect us by thy might,
>Great God our King!"

After that stirring song, Laura had this thought.

"God is America's king."

Then she reflected on what that meant.

"This is what it means to be free. It means, you have to be good... The laws of Nature and of Nature's God endow you with a right to life and liberty. Then you have to keep the laws of God, for God's law is the only thing that gives you a right to be free."

The real Laura Ingalls strongly believed God and strongly disapproved of big government. She believed in individual responsibility. After all, when a person lived on the frontier as the Ingalls did, if you didn't take care of yourself, there was no one else to take care of you. You could not get on a government welfare program.

So that essay on liberty inserted in the middle of an Independence Day celebration was Laura's position. A nation that rules itself can do so only as long as its individuals rule themselves.

John Miller's biography of Laura, *Becoming Laura Ingalls Wilder*, includes this story of what the Wilders thought about the New Deal.

"Because of the thin clay subsoil and hilly terrain on Rocky Ridge it was impossible to plow most of the acreage. Nevertheless, [Almanzo] did like to turn up an acre or so of relatively level land for oats or millet for bird feed, and he also liked to grow a little popcorn for the family. One day while he was plowing with Old Buck, his thirty-year-old Morgan, a young agent from the Department of Agriculture parked along-side the road and walked into the field to ask some questions about his farm operation. When he informed Almanzo that federal regulations prohibited him from planting more than two acres of oats, the farmer retorted that if the fellow did not immediately leave his property, he was going to go get his shotgun."

In the chapter of *Laura's Friends Remember* titled "The Politics of Laura and Almanzo," we discussed their political views.

"The foundation of Laura's thinking is individual responsibility, not government coercion. The worldwide war caused a worldwide shortage of food. Armies have to be fed, while at the same time they destroy crops with their battles. Wilson appointed Herbert Hoover, who would be president himself about a decade later, to lead America in supplying that gigantic need for food. Amazingly, Hoover did not

institute government rationing or controls. He simply asked Americans to do voluntarily all they could. That was why the Mansfield holiday party only had brown bread sandwiches and coffee, not because big government told them what to do, but because of individual responsibility.

Then we cited a statement that Laura wrote in 1918, during the Great War, that sums up her view of government and individual responsibility.

"A 'government of the people, for the people and by the people,' can be no better nor greater than the people."[83]

When the television show had an Independence Day celebration that was almost canceled because people protested higher taxes and bigger government, be confident that Laura and Almanzo would have led that protest.

In the "Troublemaker" episode, the regular teacher, Miss Beadle, was let go because she was not able to maintain order in the school. Hannibal Applewood replaced her, and the students called him 'Mr. Crabapple.' He was strict and it was his job to restore discipline. However, Mr. Applewood – with some advice from Harriet Oleson – singled Laura out as the main troublemaker. He began to punish her, and ended up expelling her from school!

The crisis was resolved when Charles Ingalls began to examine Hannibal's credentials for teaching.

Hannibal Applewood is an impressive, Charles Dickens type name, but he does not appear in Laura's books. However, Laura was really kicked out of school for being a troublemaker.

Who was the teacher who sent Laura home?

It definitely wasn't Hannibal Crabapplewood, since he didn't exist.

In the episode titled "Back to School," Eliza Jane Wilder, Almanzo's sister, became the schoolteacher in Walnut Grove. That show introduced the Wilders, with Lucy Lee Flippin as Eliza Jane and Dean Butler as Almanzo. Almanzo quickly became a focus of interest for both Laura and Nellie. Nellie thought she could win Almanzo's heart by serving him delicious food in her new restaurant. Laura was afraid that might happen, too, and volunteered to cook Nellie's meal of cinnamon chicken. However, Laura somehow managed to get the cayenne mixed up with the cinnamon so that when Almanzo ate the cayenne chicken, he and Nellie did not get off to a hot start.

Well, maybe they did, depending on how you look at it.

On the show, Miss Wilder was a gentle, sometimes intrusive woman, who eventually was willing to give up her teaching position for Laura. The real Eliza Jane Wilder was a strong willed woman. Charles Ingalls, Almanzo Wilder, and Royal Wilder all staked out homestead claims near De Smet. The homesteader had to live on the claim for most of the year for five years, and had to develop it agriculturally. At that time on the frontier, with locust plagues, hail storms, wild winters and droughts, that was no easy task.

Eliza Jane Wilder took out a homestead claim, too, and proved up on it, all by herself. Strong willed woman!

After the long, hard winter of 1880-81, Eliza Jane wrote a letter to the land commissioner about the October blizzard that began that winter.

"In Oct. a blizzard came and for three days we could not see an object ten ft from us. The R.R. were blocked for ten days. Snow in the cuts being packed like ice. After the storm ceased I went to town for flour and coal.

Our merchants had none. A carload of flour would have been there in a few hours when blockaded.

My mother took me home with her for the winter. But I left everything except my wardrobe in Dakota not expecting to be gone more than two or three months. But storm followed storm. After the middle of December I think no trains reached De Smet until May.

Many families were reported frozen to death and others lived wholly on turnips, some on wheat ground in a coffee mill."[84]

In *Farmer Boy*, strong willed Eliza Jane was kind of the Nellie Oleson of the book, but to a lesser degree. Almanzo said she was bossy and she always knew what was best. Eliza Jane did help Almanzo, though, when he got stove blacking on the wallpaper. She patched it over so that he didn't get in trouble.

When Laura and Almanzo were planning their wedding, he wanted them to have a simple, quick wedding so that Eliza Jane wouldn't take it over. They discussed that in *These Happy Golden Years*.

"If you don't, would you be willing and could you be ready to be married the last of this week, or the first of next?" he asked even more anxiously. "Don't answer till I tell you why. When I was back in Minnesota last winter, my sister Eliza started planning a big *church wedding for us. I told her we didn't want it, and to give up the idea. This morning I got a letter; she has not changed her mind. She is coming out here with my mother, to take charge of our wedding."*

"Oh, no!" Laura said.

"You know Eliza," said Almanzo. "She's headstrong, and she always was bossy..."[85]

The real Eliza Jane Wilder did teach school in De Smet, as on the show, and she did have Laura and Carrie as her pupils. Miss Wilder had already taught school back east. However, in spite of being strong willed and bossy, as a teacher Eliza Jane Wilder was quite modern. She did not believe in discipline.

Laura said that she *"had no idea how to govern a school."*[86]

Laura tried to be her friend and tried to help encourage the other young folks to be nice to her. One of the girls who was the real life model for Nellie Oleson may have put it into Miss Wilder's head that Laura and Carrie expected special treatment because their father, Charles Ingalls, was on the school board. In all the trouble she was having, Miss Wilder had a special animosity for Carrie and Laura.

One day Carrie was unconsciously rocking her desk, which had loosened from the floor. Miss Wilder became greatly agitated and ordered her to rock the desk hard. That was a rather unintelligent move by someone who was always supposed to know what was best. When weak Carrie grew tired of rocking the desk, and was in danger of fainting from the effort, Laura volunteered to rock it for her.

Miss Wilder eagerly agreed.

So Laura rocked the desk.

No, let me restate that – LAURA ROCKED THE DESK!

"Then I rocked the seat, no gentle rocking and soft sounds, but thud, thud, back and forth I sent the seat with as much noise as I could manage to make. There was no studying possible in the room and by all signs it was making teacher's head ache. I kept my eyes steadily fixed on her and rocked. She tried to stare me down but she couldn't face the blaze in my eyes and looked away.

After about twenty minutes she said we should stop rocking and go home and, with a final thud, we did."[87]

Laura and Carrie were not expelled from the school, only kicked out for that one day. However, Miss Wilder was still the same teacher as before. Boys played leap frog, threw paper wads and whistled loudly, while the girls wrote messages on their slates and passed them around.

As a schoolgirl, Miss Wilder had suffered an infestation of lice in her hair. She told her pupils, in her mawkish manner, how her classmates had teased her and called her lazy, lousy Liza Jane.

Bad move for Miss Wilder.

"One day Ida Brown drew on her slate the picture of a woman, which was anything but pretty and wrote under it, "Who would go to school to Lazy Lousy Liza Jane," Laura recalled.

"I erased what she had written and [wrote] *in its place.*

*"Going to school is lots of fun,
By laughter we have gained a ton.
For we laugh until we have a pain,
At lazy, lousy, Liza Jane."*[88]

Soon Laura's classmates were strolling down the street in De Smet singing Laura's lines as a song. That was Laura's first literary success! Miss Wilder, though, was most unimpressed.

Thankfully, Miss Wilder lasted as teacher only until the end of the month, drew her pay and went back out to her homestead.

In 1893, she married a man from Spring Valley, Minnesota, where her parents lived. She was forty-two; he had been married twice before and had six children. They resided in Crowley, Louisiana. In 1894, they had a son. Her husband died in 1899, but instead of leaving his estate to his wife Eliza Jane, as is common, he left his estate to a daughter by a previous wife. In 1904, Eliza Jane married again, only to later separate from that husband. She died in Lafayette, Louisiana in 1930 and is buried there.[89]

That was the real Miss Wilder. When Laura married Almanzo, that must have complicated matters a bit, because Laura was then the sister-in-law of lazy, lousy, Liza Jane.

It makes you wonder if they ever discussed poetry.

When Laura, Almanzo and daughter Rose first lived in Mansfield, Missouri, Mansfield did not have a full high school. At Eliza's urging, Rose went to live with Eliza in Louisiana, so she could finish high school in Crowley. It seems that Eliza Jane still knew best.

Eliza Jane died in 1930, just before Laura's first book was published in 1932. Laura received much assistance from Rose, who had lived for a year with Eliza Jane, in writing her novels. In those books – which Eliza Jane never got to read – she is consistently pictured by those who knew her well as being one notch below Nellie Oleson.

The TV show had Mr. Hannibal Applewood kicking Laura out of school, while in real life Miss Wilder did that, and then she became Laura's sister-in-law. This is another case where the real life story was more complicated than the television script.

Chapter 10

Married to Manly

When Miss Wilder first appeared on the *Little House on the Prairie* show, her brother came with her. In that episode where Eliza Jane began to teach school, Laura was smitten with the teacher's brother, Almanzo Wilder. He introduced himself to her as 'Manny.' She mistook that as 'Manly,' and they agreed that's what she would call him.

In real life, Laura's beau really was Almanzo Wilder, he was a lot older than her, and she did call him Manly. Almanzo is a bit more difficult to get out and sounds less friendly than Manly. In the show, he called her 'Beth,' from her middle name Elizabeth. Actually, Almanzo called Laura 'Bess,' which is close to Beth, if you mithpronounce it a little.

In the television series, Laura was fond of Almanzo from the get-go but it took about twenty episodes before he became interested in her. In the "Sweet Sixteen" episode, Laura became a teacher in another town. When she left, then Almanzo realized that he had feelings for Laura. At the end of the episode, he accompanied her to a church social, and at the end of that social they got more social –

He gave her their first kiss.

In real life and in *Little Town on the Prairie*, Almanzo was the one who was first smitten and Laura was the slow smiter. However, Laura did recall the first time she saw the younger Wilder boy; for whatever reason, she remembered that very clearly. It was on a day when she and Carrie took a different route home from school.

"We knew the road we traveled in the spring went through the slough still farther over and if we kept on we must come to it. So we went until we came out of the grass into a mowed place. There we saw a team hitched to a load of hay. A tall man on the ground was pitching more hay up onto the load. On top of the load a big boy or young man lay on his stomach, kicking up his heels and just as we saw them, the man on the ground pitched a great forkful of hay square on top of the other. We passed by saying good evening while the man on top of the load scrambled out from under the hay and looked at us.

As we went on, I said to Carrie, "That man on the ground was Wilder, the other must be the youngest Wilder boy." I had never seen him before."[90]

In the episode where Laura first met Almanzo, he gave her a ride on his wagon. In *Little Town on the Prairie*, Laura was headed to school, and Almanzo gave her a ride in his buggy.

"A long block from Second Street, she was hurrying along the board sidewalk, when suddenly a shining buggy pulled up beside it.

Laura looked up, surprised to see the brown Morgans. Young Mr. Wilder stood by the buggy, his cap in one hand. He held out his other hand to her and said, "Like a ride to the schoolhouse? You'll get there quicker."

He took her hand, helped her into the buggy, and stepped in beside her. Laura was almost speechless with surprise and shyness and the delight of actually riding behind those beautiful horses."[91]

Almanzo's horses were the talk of the town. Nellie Oleson lusted after a ride behind those beautiful horses. Okay – she lusted after the driver of those horses, too. So when Laura showed up at school with the horses and Almanzo, Nellie was not favorably impressed. *"Oh, I wish you could have seen her face!"* Laura's friend said of Nellie, *"when you came driving up!"*[92]

Almanzo's first "date" with Laura was when he escorted her home from church. That was not a church social, but a revival, as Laura remembered in *Pioneer Girl*.

"A revival meeting was started soon afterward and we attended nearly every night. It did not seem to me, so interesting as those we used to have in Walnut Grove, but I had a brown dress that I liked and a brown velvet turban, with a touch of red, that was very becoming. I sat demurely with Pa and Ma, well up toward the front, but I did notice the Wilder boys, Oscar Rhuel and Cap Garland always in the same place at the back of the church. To be perfectly truthful I was noticing Cap. Passing them one night on our way out, I felt a touch on my arm and someone said in my ear, "May I see you home?" It was the youngest Wilder boy, Eliza Jane's brother. In sheer astonishment I made no reply, but he took my arm and dropped into step beside me, behind Pa and Ma. Ma looked around, but Pa propelled her gently on and we went out the door and home.

I'm sure not a dozen words were said on the way, I was tongue tied wondering why he of all people should pay any attention to me. Later I learned that Oscar had dared him to ask the girl who walked

125

just behind me and they had made a bet that he would not see her home, but Oscar did not make it plain which girl he meant, so although he knew perfectly well the Wilder boy asked me as he had intended and collected the bet from Oscar, by claiming a misunderstanding. After that it was the usual thing for him to "see me home.""

Laura had no idea why Almanzo asked to see *her* home, instead of one of the other girls. From Almanzo's view, though, he not only escorted the girl of his choice, he got paid for doing so by winning a bet.

You have to keep your eye on a guy who's that clever!

These Happy Golden Years was Laura's last completed book. At the start of that novel, Pa drove Laura twelve miles from De Smet to the new school she was teaching. When the frontier was first settled, teachers were few and far between, schools were small and widely scattered so they needed a lot of teachers. A teacher was supposed to be at least sixteen to get a certificate to teach, but because of the need, Laura sneaked under the limit. She was not quite sixteen years old.

Laura did not want to be a teacher. Her mother Caroline had been a teacher for a short while before she was married. Mary had wanted to be a teacher but could not when she lost her sight. So that left Laura to be the teacher in the family, in spite of her dislike for the job.

Laura boarded with a local family near her school and their home was quarrelsome and unpleasant. Riding twelve miles on a wagon in freezing weather was a hard two to three hour trip each way, so Laura had no way to get back to the Ingalls for visits. She dreaded spending the whole weekend in that fractious home. As her first week of teaching school ended, though, Laura heard sleigh bells in the wind.

"It seemed to her that the wind had a strangely silvery sound. She listened; they all listened. She did not know what to make of it. The sky was not changed; gray, low clouds were moving fast above the prairie covered with blowing snow. The strange sound grew clearer, almost like music. Suddenly the whole air filled with a chiming of little bells. Sleigh bells!

Everyone breathed again, and smiled. Two brown horses swiftly passed the window. Laura knew them; they were Prince and Lady, young Mr. Wilder's horses!"[93]

Almanzo drove Laura home. Then he drove her back to the school on Sunday. The drive was very cold, but week after week Almanzo kept making that long trip.

For whatever reason.

The actual difference of ten years in their ages made Laura just a girl of about sixteen, while Almanzo was a mature homesteader in his mid-twenties. Laura could not believe that this mature man would actually be interested in courting her.

When he kept giving her those rides, though, in spite of the bitter cold, she began to catch on.

However, she did not share his interest. One day, on one of those cold rides, she flat out told him that he was not her beau, as she recorded in her unpublished manuscript.

"Much as I wanted to go home, I did not want to be unfair nor deceitful. I was only going with him for the sake of being home over Sunday and fully intended to stop as soon as my school was out. So

one day on the road I took fast hold on my courage and told him so. "I am only going with you," I said, "because I want to get home, but when I am home to stay, I'll not go with you any more. So if you want to stop now and save yourself these long, cold drives, you can."

"Well," he answered. "It is quite a while before school will be out anyway." It was cold, though it was nothing like the Hard Winter, still it was bad enough. The thermometer ranged from twenty to thirty below zero."[94]

After Laura told Almanzo where he stood, this happened, as Laura wrote in a magazine article in 1924, about forty years later.

"The snow was scudding low over the drifts of the white world outside the little claim shanty. It was blowing thru the cracks in its walls and forming little piles and miniature drifts on the floor and even on the desks before which several children sat, trying to study, for this abandoned claim shanty that had served as the summer home of a homesteader on the Dakota prairies was being used as a schoolhouse during the winter.

The walls were made of one thickness of wide boards with cracks between and the enormous stove that stood nearly in the center of the one room could scarcely keep out the frost tho its sides were a glowing red. The children were dressed warmly and had been allowed to gather closely around the stove following the advice of the county superintendent of schools, who on a recent visit had said that the only thing he had to say to them was to keep their feet warm.

This was my first school, I'll not say how many years ago, but I was only 16 years old and 12 miles from home during a frontier winter. I walked a mile over the unbroken snow from my boarding place to school every morning and back at night. There were only a few pupils and on this particular snowy afternoon they were restless for it was nearing 4 o'clock and tomorrow was Christmas. "Teacher" was restless, too, tho she tried not to show it for she was wondering if she could get home for Christmas day.

It was almost too cold to hope for father to come and a storm was hanging in the northwest which might mean a blizzard at any minute. Still, tomorrow was Christmas, and then there was a jingle of sleigh bells outside. A man in a huge fur coat in a sleigh full of robes passed the window. I was going home after all!

When one thinks of 12 miles now, it is in terms of motor cars and means only a few minutes. It was different then, and I'll never forget that ride. The bells made a merry jingle and the fur robes were warm, but the weather was growing colder and the snow was drifting so that the horses must break their way thru the drifts.

We were facing the strong wind and every little while he who later became "the man of the place," must stop the team, get out in the snow, and by putting his hands over each horse's nose in turn, thaw the ice from them where the breath had frozen over their nostrils. Then he would get back into the sleigh and on we'd go until once more the horse could not breathe, for the ice.

When we reached the journey's end, it was 40 degrees below zero, the snow was blowing so thickly that we could not see across the street and I was so chilled that I had to be half carried into the house. But I was home for Christmas and cold and danger were forgotten.

Such magic there is in Christmas to draw the absent ones home and if unable to go in the body the thoughts will hover there! Our hearts grow tender with childhood memories and love of kindred and we are *better throughout the year for having in spirit, become a child again at Christmas time."*[95]

Laura wondered why Almanzo again came to take her home, after she told him he would not be her beau. And he answered:

"Do you think I'm the kind of a fellow that'd leave you out there at Brewster's when you're so homesick, just because there's nothing in it for me?"[96]

With a wonderful attitude like that, how could Laura help but grow to love Almanzo?

And she did.

On the TV show, they were married in a two-part special titled "Laura Ingalls Wilder." In that episode, Eliza Jane Wilder had a romantic interest of her own. When she was reluctant to show her feelings, the gentleman became interested in someone else. Laura and Almanzo were already engaged to be married and Eliza pretended that all was well with her own romance. Almanzo lost a crop, so he postponed the wedding. Laura offered to teach school in another town to help earn money, but when Almanzo refused her offer, Laura broke off the engagement. Eliza Jane voluntarily left Walnut Grove and allowed Laura to have the teaching job she had held. Then Laura and Almanzo were married in Sleepy Eye.

In Laura's book *These Happy Golden Years*, Almanzo and Laura had a lovely courtship, much of it spent flying behind his rambunctious horses, either in a buggy or a sleigh. During those frequent and sometimes wild rides, Almanzo finally became Laura's beau.

No – the book does not record their first kiss. Nowhere does Laura mention that!

Laura and Almanzo did get married, not in Sleepy Eye, but in De Smet, in the minister's home. Eliza Jane was not there, neither were any of the Wilders, nor any of the Ingalls.

"Married WILDER-INGALLS. - At the residence of the officiating clergyman, Rev. E. Brown, August 25, 1885. Mr. Almanzo J. Wilder and Miss Laura Ingalls, both of De Smet. Thus two more of our respected young people have united in the journey of life. May their voyage be pleasant, their joys be many and their sorrows few."[97]

So the *Little House on the Prairie* TV show had Laura and Almanzo courting and getting married. The details were different, but the base was right. Laura and Almanzo did court and marry, and they stayed married until he died in 1949. Their love story was even more memorable than a scriptwriter might make up. In *Laura's Love Story*, we focused on that, not just the facts of their lives together, but the love that held them so strongly unified through some of the roughest times you can imagine. Manly and Bess were together for better, for worse, for richer, for poorer, in sickness and in health, to love and to cherish, till death did them part.

Chapter 11

The First Years of Marriage and After

After eight seasons, Michael Landon finally left his regular role on *Little House on the Prairie*. In real life, Charles Ingalls moved around a lot. On the show, though, Michael Landon moved on only after playing Charles Ingalls for eight years.

Fans were sad over Michael's exit as a regular, but Little House had run for 181 episodes, plus the pilot movie. Michael not only acted in most of them, but also wrote and directed many. In *Little House: A New Beginning*, the focus shifted from Charles and Caroline to Laura and Almanzo. As had been the pattern throughout the show, scriptwriters created the details of the stories, but certain basic premises of the shows were based in fact.

Little House episode "The Nephews" introduced Almanzo's brother Royal Wilder. In that show, Royal had two boys who were rambunctious, which made for interesting times for Laura and Almanzo, who kept them for a short while. Then in the first episode of the new series, "Times Are Changing," Charles and Caroline moved from Walnut Grove to Burr Oak, Iowa, which took them out of the series, and Royal moved into Walnut Grove, with his daughter Jenny. He was dying, he wanted to leave his daughter with Laura and Almanzo, and all of that came to pass.

Royal Wilder, older brother of Almanzo.

Royal Wilder was indeed Almanzo's older brother. In Laura's books, Royal was a major character in *Farmer Boy* and then appeared again in *The Long Winter*. He and Almanzo were both raised on a farm but had completely opposite opinions about farming. Almanzo wanted to be a farmer. Royal didn't.

And that is exactly how they turned out. Almanzo was a farmer, even though he ran into some hard times. Royal was a storekeeper. He had a homestead near De Smet but also opened a feed store in town. During the long, hard winter of 1880-81, Royal and Almanzo spent the winter in Royal's store, where they had adequate food stored away, unlike most of the people in town. In *The First Four Years*, Royal risked his own health to take care of Laura and Almanzo when they were both sick with diphtheria.

In the spring of 1890, Almanzo gave up on farming in Dakota and he and Laura headed back to Spring Valley, Minnesota, where they stayed with his folks for more than a year. Royal also left De Smet about the same time and returned to Spring Valley. Still a storekeeper at heart, he opened a variety store there. He married a widow with four children, then they had three of their own, but only one lived past infancy. Royal did not die young and leave a daughter with Almanzo and Laura. He actually lived a long life, and died in 1925 at 78 years of age.

In a two-part episode "Days of Sunshine and Shadow," several notable events befell Laura and Almanzo.

First, Almanzo became ill, and was worried about his crops. A hailstorm came up, and he was so distraught that he ran out into the hailstorm and suffered a stroke.

In real life, a hailstorm did strike Almanzo's wheat crop in the first year of their marriage, as we have already mentioned. He began to cut the wheat but decided to wait a day or two. That afternoon a monster hailstorm drove his wheat into the ground and planted it all at the wrong season.

Almanzo was not actually dumb enough to step outside when it was hailing eggs. But his neighbor was.

"It rained only a little; then hailstones began to fall, at first scattering slowly, then falling thicker and faster while the stones were larger, some of them as large as hens' eggs.

Manly and Cora (Laura's friend) watched from the windows. They could not see far into the rain and hail, but they saw Ole Larsen, across the road, come to his door and step out. Then they saw him fall, and someone reached out the door, took hold of his feet and dragged him in. Then the door shut.

"The fool," Manly said, "he got a hailstone on the head."[98]

Even though the hailstorm had destroyed most of a year's income, Almanzo was still not in a panic. In fact, after the storm had passed, he suggested to Laura that they gather up some of the piled up hailstones and make ice cream.

Laura had no appetite for ice cream.

Almanzo did have a stroke, but it had nothing to do with a hailstorm.

Laura caught diphtheria, a contagious, dangerous disease. They sent their baby daughter Rose to stay with the Ingalls while Almanzo tended to Laura. As might be expected, Almanzo caught the disease, too. Laura was sicker than her husband, but as they were recovering, apparently Almanzo went back to his farm work too quickly and suffered what they thought was a stroke.

That affected the rest of their lives, because it turned Almanzo from a tough young worker to a partially disabled man, as we discussed in *Laura's Love Story*.

"Laura was very sick, Almanzo less so, but they both gradually recovered. Once they were better, the doctor warned them to not work hard. Rose came back home to live with them. She had been gone so long that she had learned to walk at the Ingalls.

As quickly as he could, Almanzo went back to doing all the necessary chores with the animals. Against the doctor's advice, he tired himself out. One morning he got out of bed and his legs wouldn't move. A petrified Laura rubbed them fiercely to get them moving again. The diphtheria had affected his nervous system.

Almanzo was able to get around, but when he walked, he had to go around a board on the ground or he would trip over it. His fumbly hands couldn't hitch up the harness for his team of horses. Laura had to do that for him.

Gradually he got better, but for the rest of his life he was never as he was before. Almanzo had always thought that if he needed to do more, he could just work harder. Now he couldn't."[99]

In the "Days of Sunshine and Shadow" episode, where Almanzo had the stroke during the hailstorm, he became depressed and bitter over his affliction. In the show, Rose was born after his stroke, but even that did not cheer Almanzo up. Eliza Jane wanted to help by getting Almanzo a less stressful job in Minneapolis, which was her last appearance on the show. Then a tornado leveled Laura and Almanzo's home, and Laura also became depressed and bitter over their ill fortune. When Almanzo saw her like that, he turned around and his attitude improved.

In real life, Laura and Almanzo did have a daughter Rose, born about a year and a half after their marriage but before he suffered the stroke. And in real life, pioneers on the frontier did not have time for self-pity. In *Laura Ingalls' Friends Remember Her*, we talked about how they didn't cry over spilt milk.

"Little House books written by others don't sing. They tell a story, they try to be happy, and some do okay – but they don't make you bubble up inside like Laura's books do.

Amazingly, the life recounted in the Little House stories usually would be considered unhappy. When the Ingalls left the big woods of Wisconsin, they left all their family behind. When they left Kansas, they deserted a year's hard work. In Minnesota, grasshoppers destroyed their wheat crop and Mary was struck blind with illness. In South Dakota, they lived in a shanty and nearly starved to death one winter.

But Laura had the ability to be happy inside, no matter what was happening outside. The happiness in Laura's writings came from her. Not through literary sleight of hand or editorial erudition or by any writing technique, but the happiness came from Laura's spirit.

She learned that first of all from her parents' example. Time and again after some bad experience, they would say something like "all's well that ends well." Or "a miss is as good as a mile." Plus "every cloud has a silver lining." And they always tried to remember, "don't cry over spilt milk."

Actually, the pioneers faced so many difficulties, they couldn't dwell on any one problem or they would never have gotten anything done at all. So Laura picked up the custom from Charles and Caroline of making the best out of whatever was happening."

Just as Mary bore her affliction without complaining, so did Almanzo and Laura over his stroke. They did not have bitterness, just determination. Gradually Almanzo regained the use of his limbs, but he was never the same man that he was before the illness. Peggy Dennis, a friend of Laura and Almanzo, said, *"It was almost like he was club footed. He had the front of his shoe leather sewn way back and I think he did it himself. They said they thought he had suffered a stroke at one time. He always carried a heavy cane."*[100]

Guess what, though?

In "Days of Sunshine and Shadow," when their house was destroyed by a tornado –

That did not really happen to Laura and Almanzo! A tornado did strike near their house, but as Pa Ingalls might say, "A miss is as good as a mile."

Whew! They got a break on that one. The tornado didn't happen in real life.

What did happen in real life was that their house burned. But that was only after their little baby boy died.

An emotional episode of *A New Beginning* was entitled "A Child With No Name." There Laura and Almanzo's newborn baby boy died after only a few days of life. The show then focused on Laura blaming Doc Baker for the death. Rose later became ill with smallpox, so Doc Baker helped them and that resolved the problem.

In real life, Laura and Almanzo's son lived slightly longer than a few days, but no doctor could get there in time to help him. Laura wrote very little about the tragedy.

"Laura was doing her own work again one day three weeks later when the baby was taken with spasms, and he died so quickly that the doctor was too late.

To Laura, the days that followed were mercifully blurred. Her feelings were numbed and she only wanted to rest—to rest and not to think. But the work must go on. Haying had begun and Manly, Peter, and the herd boy must be fed. Rose must be cared for and all the numberless little chores attended to."[101]

That was about all she ever had to say about losing their little boy. He was born August 12, 1889, and died August 24, 1889. And no, he never had a name.

It was only a short time after that when their little house burned. The summer day was hot, so Laura had started a small fire in the kitchen for cooking and shut the door to the kitchen to keep the heat out of the rest of the house. The next thing she knew the whole kitchen was on fire. The house burned quickly and they were able to save only a few things.

Little House: A New Beginning lasted only one season. Ratings for the show did not hold up, and several subsequent special episodes wrapped up the story, with the town of Walnut Grove finally being blown up in the very last episode. Of course, the real Walnut Grove still stands and is visited by many Little House fans every year. The series showed three significant events in Laura and Almanzo's marriage. They had a little baby girl, Rose; Almanzo suffered a stroke; and they lost a little baby boy. All those things really happened.

Laura's last book was *The First Four Years*. That novel was never finished. No one even knew that it existed, until the manuscript was found in Laura's papers after her death. Why didn't she bother to complete that book, continuing the story of her and Almanzo? I asked Nava Austin why Laura didn't continue her writing, and Nava said, *"She just didn't want to write about the sad things. The first years of their marriage were rough, and she thought that was too sad to write about."*[102]

Chapter 12

Who Wuz and Who Wuzn't

Laura's daughter Rose Wilder Lane wrote two books, *Let the Hurricane Roar* and *Free Land*, which used the same stories as Laura's Little House books. Rose even wrote them at about the same time as Laura wrote hers, in the 1930's. When Laura's and Rose's books were published, Rose's were far more famous. First, *The Saturday Evening Post* serialized the two novels, and paid Rose handsomely for their use. Then they were released as successful novels and both were adapted for performance on nationwide radio. Laura's Little House books were appreciated in their own field, but they were just children's books. With the passing decades, though, the Little House books far surpassed Rose's books in general popularity and esteem.

Although Laura's and Rose's books cover the same characters and the same stories, their books are quite different. Each author took the same material and, as might be expected with different authors, went in different directions.

In a way, the same thing happened with the *Little House on the Prairie* television series. Michael Landon made the decision that to create a whole television series, he would begin with the basic facts of Laura's life, and then create other stories from that basis. That naturally leads to a different creative work – related to Laura's books, yet still standing on its own as a distinct creation.

With that in mind, we can look at the characters in the television series, and see which ones were taken directly from Laura's books, and ultimately from her life. Many were and many weren't. We can also opine on how well the actors did in their personification of the real characters.

Charles Ingalls

In both the series and the books, Charles was the second most important character, after Laura herself. Michael Landon's 'Pa Ingalls' is probably his most defining role, even though he performed longer in the Bonanza series. Is he remembered most as Little Joe or Pa Ingalls? He is beloved in both roles and the roles present a contrast, between a mischievous but good-natured young cowboy to a mature and stable father of a family. Little *House on the Prairie* has achieved greater lasting popularity than Bonanza, even though Bonanza was a bigger hit in its time, so we can assume that Pa Ingalls outgrew Little Joe in Michael's acting history.

Michael depicted Pa as a hardworking homesteader who was also very compassionate and loving toward his wife and children, a terrific husband and father. Michael, as Pa, was also quite cheerful. When you recall an image of him from the show, he likely has a somewhat impish grin sneaking across his handsome face. The scriptwriters also gave Michael a temperament where he might occasionally take a swing at someone. Perhaps that was a touch of Little Joe creeping in.

The real Pa Ingalls was in fact a hardworking homesteader who was compassionate and loving with his wife and children. Laura pictures him in a most positive way in her books as, yes, a terrific husband and father. Pa wanted to be where people weren't, though, always wanting to move farther west. He did not want to tough it out where he was; he wanted a better life somewhere else where he wasn't. In spite of that, he was well liked wherever he lived, and consistently held positions of respect and responsibility in his communities, such as being a justice of the peace or on a school board. He was not a grumpy loner by any means, and Laura recalled him as being endlessly cheerful in the face of endless trials and life tests. If we remember only one saying by Pa, he would say after some escape from near calamity, "All's well that ends well, Caroline."

Pa's fiddling personifies who he was. Laura said that they could never have made it through their rough times without Pa's fiddle. The fiddling tied the family closely together in front of a fire on a snow blown evening, and tied them together through the years with a happy approach to the realities of life. However –scriptwriters notwithstanding – Laura never showed the real Pa Ingalls taking a swing at anyone. Quite the contrary. He was a peacemaker, not a punch thrower. Laura's books, as opposed to television, don't need a lot of action to be interesting.

In *The Long Winter*, the winter was so long, with the trains blocked off by snow, that the townspeople in De Smet ran out of food. The Ingalls had several bushels of potatoes, but first ran out of butter.

Ma apologized for not having butter to go on the potatoes. "*I do wish we had some butter for them,*" she said.

Pa didn't gripe, but just appreciated the salt he had to go on them. *"Salt brings out the flavor,"* he said.

When they finally ran totally out of potatoes, Pa and Laura fussed over who would have the last one.

"Slowly they ate the last potatoes, skins and all. The blizzard was beating and scouring at the house, the winds were roaring and shrieking. The window was pale in the twilight and the stove pressed out its feeble heat against the cold.

"I'm not hungry, honest, Pa," Laura said. *"I wish you'd finish mine."*

"Eat it, Laura," Pa told her, kindly but firmly."[103]

So Michael's 'Pa' was quite true to the character of Charles Ingalls, an outstanding father and husband, with just a dash of Little Joe thrown in for spice.

Caroline Ingalls

Karen Grassle played Caroline Ingalls. This role certainly defined her acting career, although that career included many other credits and continues adding to the list at this time. Her portrayal of Ma was classic, soft spoken yet strong willed, demure but dependable. Karen has studied and worked in many areas of the world making her quite a cosmopolitan woman and her own life has been more inconstant than that of Ma Ingalls. We may allow, then, that her excellent portrayal of Ma came from her acting skills more than personal concurrence in personality. Although sometimes her smile could be beaming and her face might fill with laughter, most often we think of TV's Caroline with a subdued smile, lips together, blue eyes wide open, not openly laughing yet still pleasantly cheerful. That is her Ma Ingalls, domestic and devoted.

The real Caroline Ingalls was most patient and loving. She followed Charles through four different states, perhaps five including a possible short stint in Missouri, and lived in more than a dozen little houses, including a hole in the ground.[104] All without complaint! A main reason that Laura did not want to marry a farmer herself, even though she did, was because she had seen how hard her mother had worked. Again, all without complaint. Caroline was her daughters' teacher for most of their education, covering domestic, academic and Biblical studies. Ma Ingalls was the epitome of a loving wife and dedicated mother, so the show and Karen Grassle got that right.

Mary Ingalls

We already discussed how the show accurately pictured Mary as losing her sight in her mid-teens. The show was also generally on target in its characterization of Mary as a person. Melissa Sue Anderson played Mary as the counterpoint to boisterous Laura, and in real life, that's about the way it was.

Mary endured her loss of sight without complaint. To lose vision at the tender age of fourteen would surely be one of the greatest disappointments imaginable, affecting all future plans, including romance, marriage and family. To experience that and not be overcome by disappointment is a tremendous testament to Mary's character. Little more need be said about that. The way she lived her life after losing her sight showed who Mary was.

Melissa Anderson played Mary on the show as a good, dependable, responsible young lady. If Laura was a tomboy, then Mary was a kitten-girl.

Melissa and her husband and children moved to Montreal, Canada, far away from the Hollywood hype, and even became Canadian citizens. As her family matures, she looks to again become more active in the acting field, after taking time through the years to raise her children.

When Melissa was auditioning for the Little House series, this happened.

"So you've probably read the books that this movie is based on, then?" Al said.

I told him, "I don't know what books you mean. My agent said she thought it was a Western."

"Ah, well, it is, a bit," Al said. "A pioneer Western you could say: Little House on the Prairie?"

I bounced up and down in my chair. "I've read all of those books. I loved them. That's what this is? Neat!"

The executives laughed at that and asked me if I knew which role I was being considered for.

"Oh, I'm sure it must be Mary, right?"

"You got it, Melissa," Al said. "You certainly have the blue eyes for it."[105]

Wouldn't you know that the nice girl who would play Mary would already be a Little House girl?

Laura Ingalls

We have already talked about how feisty Laura was, on the show and in real life. Here's one more example, when Laura wrote a story about herself.

"All the world is queer, except thee and me," said the old Quaker to his wife, "and sometimes, I think thee is a little queer."

The Man of the Place once bought me a patent churn. "Now," said he, "Throw away that old dash churn. This churn will bring the butter in 3 minutes." It was very kind of him. He had bought the churn to please me and to lighten my work, but I looked upon it with a little suspicion. There was only one handle to turn and opposite it was a place to attach the power from a small engine. We had no engine so the churning must needs be done with one hand, while the other steadied the churn and held it down. It was hard to do, but the butter did come quickly and I would have used it anyway because the Man of the Place had been so kind.

The tin paddles which worked the cream were sharp on the edges and they were attached to the shaft by a screw which was supposed to be loosened to remove the paddles for washing, but I could never loosen it and usually cut my hands on the sharp tin. However, I used the new churn, one hand holding it down to the floor with grim resolution, while the other turned the handle with the strength of despair when the cream thickened. Finally it seemed that I could use it no longer. "I wish you would bring in my old dash churn," I said to the Man of the Place. "I believe it is easier to use than this after all."

"Oh!" said he: "you can churn in 3 minutes with this and the old one takes half a day. Put one end of a board on the churn and the other on a chair and sit on the board, then you can hold the churn down easily!" And so when I churned I sat on a board in the correct mode for horseback riding and tho the churn bucked some I managed to hold my seat. "I wish," said I to the Man of the Place, "you would bring in my old dash churn." (It was where I could not get it.) "I cut my hands on these paddles every time I wash them."

"Oh, pshaw!" said he, "you can churn with this churn in 3 minutes—"

One day when the churn had been particularly annoying and had cut my hand badly, I took the mechanism of the churn, handle, shaft, wheels and paddles all attached, to the side door which is quite high from the ground and threw it as far as I could. It struck on the handle, rebounded, landed on the paddles, crumpled and lay still and I went out and kicked it before I picked it up. The handle was broken off, the shaft was bent and the paddles were a wreck.

"I wish," I remarked casually to the Man of the Place, "that you would bring in my old dash churn. I want to churn this morning."

"Oh, use the churn you have," said he. "You can churn in 3 minutes with it. What's the use to spend half a day—"

"I can't," I interrupted. "It's broken."

"Why how did that happen?" he asked.

"I dropped it- just as far as I could," I answered in a small voice and he replied regretfully, "I wish I had known that you did not want to use it, I would like to have the wheels and shaft, but they're ruined now."

This is not intended as a condemnation of the patent churns – there are good ones – but as a reminder that being new and patented is no proof that a thing is better, even tho some smooth tongued agent has persuaded us that it will save time.

Also, as the old Quaker remarked to his wife, "Sometimes, I think thee is a little queer."[106]

Since Laura poked fun at herself in this story, that shows she wasn't too full of herself. Just don't mess with her churn.

The next article of hers shows that she also tried to go out of her way to be tactful.

October 5, 1916, Laura Ingalls Wilder

"You have so much tact and can get along with people so well," said a friend to me once. Then after a thoughtful pause she added, "But I never could see any difference between tact and trickery." Upon my assuring her that there was no difference, she pursued the subject further.

"Now I have no tact whatever, but speak plainly," she said pridefully. "The Scotch people are, I think, the most tactful and the Scotch, you know, are the trickiest nation in the world."

As I am of Scotch descent, I could restrain my merriment no longer and when I recovered enough to say, "You are right, I am Scotch," she smiled ruefully and said, "I told you I had no tact."

Tact does for life just what lubricating oil does for machinery. It makes the wheels run smoothly and without it there is a great deal of friction and possibly a breakdown. Many a car on the way of life fails to make the trip as expected for lack of this lubricant. Tact is a quality that may be acquired. It is only the other way of seeing and presenting a subject. There are always two sides to a thing, you know, and if one side is disagreeable the reverse is quite apt to be very pleasant. The tactful person may see both sides but uses the pleasant one.

"Your teeth are so pretty when you keep them white," said Ida to Stella; which of course was equal to saying that Stella's teeth were ugly when she did not keep them clean, as frequently happened, but Stella left her friend with the feeling that she had been complimented and also with the shamed resolve that she would keep those pretty teeth white.

Tom's shoulders were becoming inclined to droop a little. To be sure he was a little older than he used to be and sometimes very tired, but the droop was really caused more by carelessness than by anything else. When Jane came home from a visit to a friend whose husband was very round shouldered indeed, she noticed more plainly than usual the beginning of the habit in Tom.

Choosing a moment when he straightened to his full height and squared his shoulders, she said: "Oh, Tom! I'm so glad you are tall and straight, not round shouldered like Dick. He is growing worse every day until it is becoming a positive deformity with him." And Tom was glad she had not observed the tendency in his shoulders and thereafter their straightness was noticeable.

Jane might have chosen a moment when Tom's shoulders were drooping and with perfect truthfulness have said: "Tom! You are getting to be round shouldered and ugly like Dick. In a little while you will look like a hunchback."

Tom would have felt hurt and resentful and probably would have retorted, "Well you're getting older and uglier too," or something like that, and his hurt pride and vanity would have been a hindrance instead of a help to improvement.

The children, of course, get their bad tempers from their fathers, but I think we get our vanity from Adam, for we all have it, men and women alike, and like most things it is good when rightly used.

Tact may be trickery but after all I think I prefer the dictionary definition- "nice discernment." To be tactful one has only to discern or distinguish, or in other words to see, nicely and speak and act accordingly.

My sympathy just now, however, is very much with the persons who seem to be unable to say the right thing at the proper time. In spite of oneself there are times when one's mental fingers seem to be all thumbs. At a little gathering, not long ago, I differed with the hostess on a question which arose and disagreed with just a shade more warmth than I intended. I resolved to make it up by being a little extra sweet to her before I left. The refreshments served were so dainty and delicious that I thought I would find some pleasant way to tell her so. But alas! As it was a very hot day, ice water was served after the little luncheon and I found myself looking sweetly into my hostess's face and heard myself say, "Oh, wasn't that water good." What could one do after that, but murmur the conventional, "Such a pleasant afternoon," at leaving and depart feeling like a little girl who has blundered at her first party."

Melissa Gilbert portrayed Laura on the show as feisty, fun, friendly and most of all lovable. Melissa's autobiography is titled *Prairie Tale: A Memoir*. It was a *New York Times* bestseller and *Entertainment Weekly* had this to say about the book. *"Hold onto your sunbonnets... [Gilbert's] autobiography is no clean-cut family drama: It's chockablock with juicy tidbits."*

That degree of what we might call feistiness actually exceeds the real Laura. Laura was a small farm wife for almost all her married life, was extremely happy with that role, and overall lived a very constant life, culminating in the classic books that she, Almanzo and Rose created. Overall, though, the show again excelled in its characterizations, and Melissa Gilbert's Laura is certainly one of the most likeable characters in television history.

Carrie and Grace Ingalls

Carrie and Grace were characterized in the show as little sisters, which is about the same way they were approached in the books, so I suppose we can say that the show's characterization of them was accurate. A work can have only so many important roles and Carrie and Grace were not dominant characters in either the books or the show. Identical twins Lindsay and Sidney Greenbush played Carrie, and identical twins Wendi Lou and Brenda Lea Turnbaugh played Grace. In the 90-minute episode "The Godsister," Carrie missed Pa when he was away for several weeks, so she invented an imaginary friend like herself. Then both Lindsay and Sidney Greenbush were onscreen at the same time. Both sets of twins left acting after the end of the series, although all are still fondly remembered for their roles in the Little House series.

Almanzo Wilder

Almanzo did not enter the television series until it was more than halfway through its run. He was introduced at the beginning of the sixth season and, as you know, was a tall, handsome dude. Dean Butler, that tall, handsome dude, actually tried to be Adam Kendall – not Laura Ingalls' husband, but Mary Ingalls' husband.

The *Miami News*, in a July 12, 1982 article titled, "Dean Butler hits it big in new shot at Little House," revealed how Dean tried to wed the other sister.

"One of the parts [Dean] auditioned for was Adam Kendall in "Little House on the Prairie." He didn't get the part. But casting director Susan Sukman remembered him when she needed a husband for Laura Ingalls."

"They flew me down from college to meet Michael Landon," [Dean] said. "I was told that whatever I did, don't act for him. So I read for Mike in a very natural way. That's the way he likes it. Before I walked out the door, he asked me what I'd be doing in May. I said I'd be doing my final exams."

Two days after he graduated from college, he started his role in "Little House.""[107]

If an actor plays a leading man on TV, does he have to be tall, blond and handsome? Perhaps that is one of the characteristics of the medium, and no matter which scene or story might be involved, there is no getting around the fact that Dean Butler was a handsome leading man, articulate and well spoken, debonair and dashing. Actually, had he not been so, you probably would not have enjoyed watching him on the screen.

Dean's Almanzo was certainly lively and likeable, and, owing mostly to the medium, the character is a bit more dramatic than the real fellow usually was.

The real Almanzo was rather lively and definitely likeable, too, but in a different way.

He was a farmer.

Is that the opposite of a handsome, leading man?

Probably.

He lost his hair somewhere between marriage and old age, as many men do, Dean Butler excepted. He was not a man of words; in fact, he didn't even like going to school. He far preferred to stay home and work with the calves and colts, or even to plant carrots. He was not tall, standing only a few inches above Laura, who was known to her Pa as Half-Pint.

He was a farmer through and through, with calloused hands, sunburned face, and wiry frame. Those tough hands were talented, able to make a cutter sleigh to take cute little Laura sleighing around town, or a delicate lap desk for her to write on. He was a man of great patience. When Laura told him that he was not her beau, he kept acting like he was – until he was.

He was a man of real character. During the unbelievably hard winter of 1880-81, the town of De Smet, among many others, nearly ran out of food. Laura wrote this article about that time, and about her man Almanzo.

"That winter, known still among the old residents as "the hard winter," we demonstrated that wheat could be ground in an ordinary coffee mill and used for bread making. Prepared in that way it was the staff of life for the whole community. The grinding at home was not done to reduce the cost of living, but simply to make living possible.

De Smet was built as the railroad went thru, out in the midst of the great Dakota prairies far ahead of the farming settlements, and this first winter of its existence it was isolated from the rest of the world from December 1 until May 10 by the fearful blizzards that piled the snow 40 feet deep on the railroad tracks. The trains could not get thru. It was at the risk of life that anyone went even a mile from shelter, for the storms came up so quickly and were so fierce it was literally impossible to see the hand before the face and men have frozen to death within a few feet of shelter because they did not know they were near safety.

The small supply of provisions in town soon gave out. The last sack of flour sold for $50 and the last of the sugar at $1 a pound. There was some wheat on hand, brought in the fall before for seed in the spring, and two young men dared to drive 15 miles to where a solitary settler had also laid in his supply of seed wheat. They brought it in on sleds. There were no mills in town or country so this wheat was all ground in the homes in coffee mills. Everybody ground wheat, even the children taking their turns, and the resultant whole wheat flour made good bread. It was also a healthful food and there was not a case of sickness in town that winter.

It may be that the generous supply of fresh air had something to do with the general good health. Air is certainly fresh when the thermometer registers all the way from 15 to 40 degrees below zero with the wind moving at blizzard speed. In the main street of the town, snow drifts in one night were piled as high as the second stories of the houses and packed hard enough to drive over and the next night the wind might sweep the spot bare. As the houses were new and unfinished so that the snow would blow in and drift across us as we slept, fresh air was not a luxury. The houses were not overheated in daytime either, for the fuel gave out early in the winter and all there was left with which to cook and keep warm was the long prairie hay. A handful of hay was twisted into a rope, then doubled and allowed to twist back on itself and the two ends tied together in a knot, making what we called "a stick of hay."

It was a busy job to keep a supply of these "sticks" ahead of a hungry stove when the storm winds were blowing, but every one took his turn good naturedly. There is something in living close to the great elemental forces of nature that causes people to rise above small annoyances and discomforts."[108]

It is almost impossible for us to conceive of the situation that they faced that year. The new town had few provisions, like food and fuel, to make it through the winter. No crops had been raised there. There were few trees for firewood. No one, people or stores, had much of a stock of anything. They were counting on the trains – the new, just built, reliable railroad! – to keep them supplied through their first winter there.

Then it snowed so much that the trains could not break through the snow. One train tried, when a mammoth steam engine backed up and bore full throttle into a cut in the knoll filled with icy packed snow. The snow stopped it cold, and the hot engine melted the snow next to it, which then froze back around it.

Notice again what Laura said about the conditions, remembering that this account was not written for drama, but for information.

"It was at the risk of life that anyone went even a mile from shelter, for the storms came up so quickly and were so fierce it was literally impossible to see the hand before the face and men have frozen to death within a few feet of shelter because they did not know they were near safety."

Don't underestimate the danger she described. Many people died in those storms. Many cattle ranchers were wiped out as their herds froze to death. Schoolchildren died on the way home from school.

In those dangerous conditions, then, *"two young men dared to drive 15 miles to where a solitary settler had also laid in his supply of seed wheat."* That wheat helped the townspeople, including Caroline, Charles, Mary, Laura, Carrie and Grace Ingalls, keep from starving that winter. And one of those two brave young men, who frosted their feet on that trip, was Almanzo Wilder. Laura doesn't mention his name in this article because to do so would be immodest and indiscrete, but her husband risked his life to help save the town.

That's a real leading man, isn't it?

Well, that was the real life Almanzo Wilder.

Nellie Oleson

In Laura's books, Nellie Oleson was based on a girl named Nellie Owens, with bits of a couple of other girls thrown in. Perhaps the reason for that is because no one girl, all by herself, could be as stinky as Nellie was. In the Little House books, Nellie was a recurring character. Not as much as in the show, but the books are very cheerful and uplifting, so you can't mix too much Nellie in with that.

Nellie was acted by Alison Arngrim. Alison performed the part so well that she became an American icon of sorts, picturing the spoiled, peevish child. Decades later in 2009, *World Magazine* ran an article titled "Are you raising a Nellie

Oleson?" and the readers were presumed to know what that means. It may well be that of all the actors in the series, Nellie's character made the strongest, most memorable impression.

Alison Arngrim first tried out for the part of Laura. Can you picture the girl who sneered "Country girls!" being the country girl?

Next Alison read for the part of Mary. Yes, that's right. The girl who became Nellie Oleson wanted to play the part of meek, mild Mary. In the series, Mary is most remembered for the episodes "I'll Be Waving As You Drive Away," where she lost her sight and came to accept that lot. Melissa Sue Anderson was outstanding in that part, and it's quite a stretch to see Nellie Oleson/Arngrim calmly sitting in a rocker, resigned to her fate.

Once again, the casting department for the series knew what they were doing. Alison was not Laura or Mary. She was Nellie Oleson.

"I had been working off and on since I was very little," Alison recalled, *"commercials and episodic things, and I got this audition, and what's interesting is I originally went in and they said "we're making a series, we're going to do those "Little House" books. And I hadn't read the Little House books."*

Unlike Michael Landon's daughter and Ed Friendly's daughter and Melissa Gilbert and Melissa Sue Anderson, Alison was not a Little House girl. She had no connection to the books.

Alison remembered that the TV producers *"had me come back and I read for the part of Laura, and I remember thinking "Oh no, I'm not going to get this."*

Alison sensed that she was not right for Laura.

"Then I read for the part of Mary. Yeah, right."

Alison absolutely knew she was not Mary Ingalls. *"Yeah, right."*

"Then they called me back and I thought "Well, how many people do they have on this show?" And I read the part of Nellie."

Notice that the TV producers sought Alison out for the part of Nellie. They called her.

"And as I said, I read the first few pages, "this girl's the bitch." And I read the part for my father before the audition and he said "Don't change [a] thing" and I went and I was hired on the spot. So apparently something was coming through. And I enjoyed it enormously, but I just auditioned and got it."

Something was coming through, Alison said. Perhaps when the little girl was sitting there thinking, *"this girl's the bitch,"* that was coming through. That same approach may have come through in Alison's well known autobiography, Confessions of a Prairie Bitch: How I Survived Nellie Oleson and Learned to Love Being Hated.

Then, when she played Nellie, this came through.

"The episodes where I would scream and yell and break everything in the place and scream that I'm going to kill someone. Do you have any idea how good that felt? I would come home at the end of the day

to fall into bed, I was so relaxed. It was the most incredible therapy. I got to be horrible and scream, I didn't have to be nice to people, I could break things. I could let it all out."[109]

After her seven seasons on Little House, to the television audience Alison was Nellie Oleson. She never received any other TV series offers.

"When you come off a series, especially where you're a child star and you come off of "Little House" and they're like "Oh yes, that was a lovely show, but we're not doing any 1800s TV right now." And there was absolutely a sense of typecasting."

Alison Arngrim was always going to be Nellie Oleson. However, in a possible divergence from Nellie's character, Alison was not glum over Nellie's pall on her acting career.

"I can't really complain, I mean, yes, I've been typecast and a lot of people in my position would say, "Oh it's so awful, I'm so bitter I've been typecast." But I was typecast being on one of the most fabulous shows ever made and as one of the most wonderful characters. So I'm not going to cry."

Alison did not wind up with the leading role on the show, but she did wind up with one of the all time best-known roles in American television, and she helped make it that way. Ali made Nellie what she is.

Harriet, Nels and Willie Oleson

In the television series, Mrs. Oleson was Nellie all grown up, or conversely, Nellie was a little Harriet. Nels Oleson was a tormented husband, constantly seeking to balance his wife's selfish pursuits. Katherine MacGregor was unforgettable as

Harriet, Richard Bull was forgivable as Nels, and Jonathan Gilbert was an often irritating but sometimes likeable Willie. In real life, Jonathan is the adopted brother of Melissa Gilbert.

While the books emphasized Nellie as Nellie, they did not emphasize Mr. or Mrs. Oleson. They appeared in *On the Banks of Plum Creek* in the chapter titled "Town Party." Mary, Laura and the other little girls from the school went through Oleson's store into their living quarters behind the store. Under her bare feet, Laura felt the heavy, colored cloth that covered the floor. Carpet was a new thing for her, for she had once lived in a dugout with a dirt floor. Laura marveled at the dining and bedroom furniture, fine pictures on the walls and lace curtains draping from the windows. Mrs. Oleson forced Willie let the other children play with some of his toys. When Laura sat down by herself because Nellie was obnoxiously rude, Mrs. Oleson gave her some wonderful books for her entertainment.

As for Mr. Oleson, when Willie made fun of Mary and Laura, Mr. Oleson told him to shut up. He also offered to let Mary and Laura have a penny pencil, when they did not have the penny to pay for it. They refused.

Laura's books do not call the Olesons by their first names, and they are not presented in a particularly negative way, other than raising bratty kids. But I guess that is pretty negative.

Willie Oleson is written up briefly as the male counterpart to Nellie.

"Suddenly the back door of the store burst open, and Nellie Oleson and her little brother Willie came bouncing in. Nellie's nose

wrinkled at Laura and Mary, and Willie yahed at them: "Yah! Yah! Long-legged snipes!"

"Shut up, Willie," Mr. Oleson said. But Willie did not shut up. He went on saying: "Snipes! Snipes!"

Nellie flounced by Mary and Laura, and dug her hands into a pail of candy. Willie dug into the other pail. They grabbed all the candy they could hold and stood cramming it into their mouths. They stood in front of Mary and Laura, looking at them, and did not offer them even one piece."[110]

The tone of Laura's books is not confrontational at all, but very uplifting and pleasant. Nellie is the prime antagonist, Pa's fiddle is the prime palliative, and the negative Olesons are hardly mentioned at all. The scriptwriters for the TV series took the Olesons as Laura briefly wrote them up, and then built on that foundation.

Are you disappointed that Laura basically left Harriet Oleson out of her books? Be careful what you wish for!

Mr. Edwards

In the show, Isaiah Edwards is a mainstay. He is a good friend of Charles and, with his personal struggles, a source of many storylines.

Mr. Edwards first appeared in the books in Little House on the Prairie. In Kansas, he was a neighbor of theirs, only two miles away. He helped Pa build his cabin and dig his well. Laura described him as a lean, tall and tanned man, who wore a coonskin cap. Mr. Edwards described himself as a wildcat from Tennessee. In a bit of a departure from the normal etiquette of Laura's books for children, she said that Mr. Edwards could spit tobacco juice farther than anyone, and this talent was carried over into the show.

Laura's favorite memory of Mr. Edwards was when he crossed a swollen creek to bring the girls some things he had gotten them for Christmas. This story appeared in the Little House pilot movie, very much in the original form. Also in the episode "A Christmas They Never Forgot," Laura recalled that Christmas in Kansas with Mr. Edwards.

In her straightforward memories in *Pioneer Girl*, Mr. Edwards was Mr. Brown.

"Indians didn't come any more after the fire and we were all very happy and quiet until before Christmas it began to rain. It rained so much that Pa couldn't go to town to tell Santa Clause what we wanted for Christmas. He said the creek was up so high he was afraid Santa Clause couldn't get across it to bring us anything.

But when we waked up on Christmas morning our stockings were hanging on the back of a chair by our bed and out of the top of each stood a bright, shining new tin cup. Farther down was a long, flat stick of red and white striped peppermint candy all beautifully notched along each edge. Mr. Brown the neighbor from across the creek stood looking at us. He said Santa Clause couldn't cross the creek the night before so he left the presents with him and he swam over that morning."

In the novels, when the Ingalls left Kansas and traveled back to Wisconsin, Mr. Edwards headed south, not reappearing in the story until they spent the winter on Silver Lake. There Mr. Edwards helped Pa get in front of a big crowd to file his homestead claim.

In *The Long Winter*, Mr. Edwards visited the Ingalls again. By then, he had a wife and was preparing to head farther west. When he saw that Mary had become blind, he left her this.

"Mary lifted her handkerchief from her lap, as she started to leave the table, and something fluttered to the floor. Ma stooped to pick it up. She stood holding it, speechless, and Laura cried, "Mary! A twenty dollar— You dropped a twenty dollar bill!"

"I couldn't!" Mary exclaimed.

"That Edwards," said Pa."[111]

That was about it for Mr. Edwards in the books. His first name was never cited. He was just Mr. Edwards. To Little House TV fans, of course, Isaiah Edwards is Victor French, grizzled and gruff but friendly and funny. Although he barely exists in the books, in the series he is one of the most important and oft appearing characters. He was Pa Ingalls' closest friend, and that portrayal may have been due to the fact that, in real life, Victor and Michael Landon were close friends.

Reverend Alden

As we cited earlier, the Congregational Church preacher did appear a few times in Laura's novels, and in her real life. Again, he was far more prominent in the show than in the novels. Dabbs Greer played the role of the preacher in the show for all nine seasons. Did he do well in the role of a preacher? He must have, because he was also a preacher in such varied series as *The Dick Van Dyke Show* and *The Brady Bunch*, among others. The man who portrayed the Reverend Alden in a kind, comforting way in Little House just seemed like a preacher.

Miss Eva Beadle, the schoolteacher

In *On the Banks of Plum Creek*, she was the schoolteacher in Walnut Grove school. When Laura and Mary did not want to go back to Oleson's store to buy a penny pencil, *"They bought it at Mr. Beadle's store and post-office, where Teacher lived, and that morning they walked on to school with Teacher."*[112]

When the Ingalls moved on to Dakota, Miss Beadle was left behind in Walnut Grove, but she probably didn't mind.

Eliza Jane Wilder

As discussed earlier, Almanzo's sister Eliza Jane Wilder was a bit more dramatic in real life than the show portrayed. Lucy Lee Flippin played Eliza Jane as a somewhat intrusive relative, as when she wanted to get Almanzo a less stressful job in Minneapolis, although she did have her good side, as when she left Walnut Grove so that Laura could be the teacher there. Lucy Flippin's portrayal of Eliza Jane was certainly memorable. The character she created just sticks in your mind, even though she was not one of the dominant characters in the show. Perhaps in that complexity of a taking and giving personality, she reflected fairly accurately the original character.

Royal Wilder

Royal is pictured in the books naturally as Almanzo's older brother but also his buddy. His most notable appearance was in The First Four Years when he risked himself to care for Laura and Almanzo. In Farmer Boy he is a frequent companion of Almanzo, but his character in the books is not extensively developed, other than being around his younger brother.

In the show, Royal was first portrayed by Woody Eney, as the father of two uncontrolled sons, and then by Nicholas Pryor, as the father of Jenny, who was taken in by Laura and Almanzo when Royal died. These portrayals are a bit contradictory and had little relation to the real Royal, other than in name.

Dr. Hiram Baker, Walnut Grove physician

A doctor came to treat Ma when she was ill at Plum Creek, but he was not named. The family had no real personal interaction with him in the book. The scriptwriters thus created the character of Doc Baker.

Lars Hanson, owner of the Hanson Lumber Mill

As mentioned earlier, Pa bought his farm near Walnut Grove from a Mr. Hanson, who then left the area and the story. The lumber mill owner Lars Hanson was originated by the show.

That leaves many characters who appeared in the show but not in the books. The whole Little House series had 203 episodes plus four longer movies, while Laura wrote only nine books. The pilot movie basically covered Laura's *Little House on the Prairie* book, so from that we might equate each normal episode with half a book and each longer movie with one book. That means, then, that while Laura wrote nine Little House books, the scriptwriters wrote the equivalent of over a hundred Little House books.

Whew! No wonder they introduced a few new characters!

Some of those many characters they created were –

Albert Ingalls, adopted son of Caroline and Charles Ingalls;

Grace Snider, who married Isaiah Edwards and together adopted three orphans;

Adam Kendall, Mary's husband. Mary never actually married;

John Carter, the blacksmith, and his family;

Jenny Wilder, Royal's daughter, who lived with Laura and Almanzo after Royal died;

Nancy Oleson, who was created to fulfill the impolite but important function of Nellie Oleson, after Nellie/Allison Arngrim grew up.

As we have seen, the most important characters in Laura's books, and life, were also included in the television series. Basically all other characters in the show were created by the scriptwriters. They had to do that, as Michael Landon had foreseen, because they wrote more than ten times the volume that Laura did.

Chapter 13

Michael to Laura, Son and Father

Here's a riddle.

How was Michael Landon both Laura's son and father?

Michael Landon created a whole series based on Laura Ingalls Wilder's stories. In that sense, he was her son, her offspring. Yet on the show, Michael was Laura's father.

Here's another riddle. How are the Little House books and the show the same, different, and the same?

In the episode of *Little House: A New Beginning*, titled "Once Upon A Time," Laura entered a writing contest. She wrote a book that greatly moved Almanzo and Jenny, their niece in the show. This is what she read to them.

"She looked at Ma gently rocking and knitting. She thought to herself, 'This is now.' She was glad that the cozy house, and Pa, and Ma, and the firelight, and the music, was now. It could not be forgotten, she thought, because now is now. It can never be a long time ago."

That is from the end of Laura's first book, *Little House in the Big Woods*, as we quoted before. Quite poetic, don't you think?

In this episode, a publisher agreed to publish Laura's book, but wanted to alter it substantially, to make it more exciting. Hollywood producers always do the same thing with the Bible, you know. Jenny convinced Laura that the new book was a lie, so Laura refused to let them publish her book.

The drama ended with a flash forward, showing Michael Landon's real daughter Shawna running into a modern day library and reading Laura's book *Little House on the Prairie*. In a voice over, Michael said that *"forty years later Laura had her book published... This time no one made any changes."*

There is a touch of irony there. In fact, a publisher did reject Laura's first book. She called that manuscript *Pioneer Girl* and it was more of a straightforward telling of her memories and family stories, without drama and formal structuring. The publisher felt that it needed more interest, but instead of the publisher rewriting it, Laura turned to her daughter Rose to help her rework the book. They took part of *Pioneer Girl* and rewrote it into *Little House in the Big Woods*, which was then successfully published. As we noted earlier, they did make some minor factual changes in the story, such as exactly when Laura lived in Wisconsin and Kansas, to simplify the story flow.

There is another irony in this episode where Laura refused to allow her altered book to be published. That is the same debate that Michael had with Ed Friendly, whether to follow the story of the books closely or just use them as a base for further stories. Michael did alter the original story and created the Little House series that became so popular.

Back to our riddle – How are the Little House books and the show the same, different, and the same?

The books and the show are the same, in that they have many of the same characters.

The books and the show are different, in that most of the show's episodes are original.

And the books and the show are the same –

How?

Laura's books have never been out of print. All through the Roosevelt Depression years, through World War II, through the coming of television in the 1950's, through the Beatles and the Vietnam War, and through all the Harry Potter and vampire times since then, her books have continued to sell. They have become enduring classics in American literature, not just with critics and academics, but with common American families. They are also popular with families around the world, as the books have been translated into a number of different languages.

In this age of iPads and hip-hop, why do these old-fashioned books still sell?

When the *Little House on the Prairie* pilot movie was shown on NBC, it was the highest rated Movie of the Week they had ever shown. Every year for nine seasons, the series was in the top thirty shows on television, and twice made the top ten.

Nielsen ratings

Season 1 (1974–75): #13
Season 2 (1975–76): #16
Season 3 (1976–77): #7
Season 4 (1977–78): #14

Season 5 (1978–79): #16
Season 6 (1979–80): #10
Season 7 (1980–81): #25
Season 8 (1981–82): #29
Season 9 (1982–83): #28[113]

Former President Ronald Reagan, a former actor himself, once said that *Little House on the Prairie* was his favorite television program.[114] Many people agreed with him.

However, the broadness of its popularity did not match the depth of its appeal. Viewers grew emotionally involved with the characters on the show, so much so that TV Guide rated Charles Ingalls as the Fourth Greatest TV Dad of all time. In a love/hate relationship, Nellie Oleson was crowned No. 3 of TV's Top 10 Biggest Brats.

And you thought she was number one!

About four decades later, the show still appears regularly on television, often not just one day a week, but five days a week! Decade after decade the show continues to run. When one channel or syndicator drops it, another one picks it up. When we first began watching the show about 1975, I was a young, strapping man in my twenties. As I write this, I am an old, stooping man in my sixties, yet the Little House show continues on television. Would that I had aged so well!

Perhaps that's what they mean when they say, 'The show must go on!' *Little House on the Prairie* TV show just goes on and on.

The show's continuing popularity means that every new generation brings new Little House fans who discover the

Ingalls and Walnut Grove afresh for themselves. The series has a timeless value whose appeal stretches through the years and through different generations and through earthshaking societal shifts.

Laura's Little House books stay popular through the years. Michael's Little House TV show stays popular through the years. They both have a depth of appeal that goes beyond statistical numbers. The people who like this Little House stuff *really* like it!

What is it that makes people continue to like both these Little House creations, even though their stories differ greatly?

The books and the show are the same, based on the same characters; and different, because they have different stories; and the same, because they share a common bond.

What is that common bond?

Values.

The TV series is described as being about faith, family and friends. Laura's books are exactly the same way – faith, family and friends.

This is the greatest similarity of all between the books and the show. They both try to lift the spirit, to be positive in a negative world, to give life meaning in a sometimes meaningless maze. In a hedonistic world, where nearly everyone tries to root out everyone else, the books and the show emphasize not being selfish. In a time when dirty material is common and almost mandatory, they present clean stories. In a society where families are torn apart by money and malice and even electronic gadgets, they both hold the family together.

Little House books and shows are still popular today because there is a drought of such material. When Laura and Almanzo were first married, they planted ten acres of trees on the dry, windswept prairie. Then drought hit. Almanzo carried buckets and buckets of water to pour on those suffering saplings. We are like that today – we are in a drought of values. Reading Laura's books or watching Michael's shows is like pouring buckets of fresh water on us, soothing the dryness of the times, refreshing us with a moment of happiness in a desert of despair.

Almanzo's little trees were starved for water. People today are starved for things of real value, and both the books and the shows shower us with meaning in life.

Here is one of the most often quoted sections of Laura's articles.

"As the years pass, I am coming more and more to understand that it is the common, everyday blessings of our common everyday lives for which we should be particularly grateful. They are the things that fill our lives with comfort and our hearts with gladness–just the pure air to breathe and the strength to breathe it; just warmth and shelter and home folks; just plain food that gives us strength; the bright sunshine on a cold day and a cool breeze when the day is warm."[115]

Michael's shows agreed with that quote from Laura. The books and the series had that in common. The simplest things in life *are* the greatest things in life. Take that to the Little House!

That's why we drink forty-year-old water. Things have changed. There are no more movies like *Sound of Music* or *Oklahoma, My Fair Lady* or *South Pacific*, where the music and the scenery and the story make our spirits soar. No TV shows like *I Love Lucy* or *Honeymooners*, where we can laugh without being slimed. No new major network Little House type shows, where we can unashamedly and unabashedly love one another.

The Little House values are what the Little House books and shows have most in common. When you watch the shows and read the books, appreciate that fact most of all. Laura and Michael wrote with different pens, but they shared the same ink.

Well, Laura wrote with a pencil, but you know what I mean.

This book about *The Real Laura* is written to fans of the Little House TV show who have not read Laura's books and are interested in the connection between the two. In giving talks to Little House fans, many more people have watched the show than have read the books. Almost everyone who has read the books has watched the show, at least sometimes. Relatively few of those who have watched the show have read the books.

So although this book is for those who have not read the books, let me be so presumptuous as to now give you some advice.

Read the books!

They are called children's books, and indeed, they are easy enough for children to read. But I think they are more correctly described as family books, because they have been read many times by Ma's and Pa's and their little ones, sitting around a flickering blaze, sharing the warmth of a fireside and family love together. Even if your children have all grown up, reading these books will still give you the picture of that family love that you appreciate so much.

Yes, read Laura's books!

They are the story of her life, beginning about 1870 and stretching for the next two decades. But these books are more than just a history of one family and more than just a treatise on family values – they are a history of America itself, an America that was and will never be again. The Ingalls were a fine, fine family, but they were not an uncommon family for the times. Living with that family in Laura's books lets you live as an American pioneer and become one with the many people who helped make America great.

That is the real Laura. A person of principle, of purpose, of passion and of purity. *A person of values.* And that is the real Little House show, a production that varied the stories, but most of all, tried to uphold certain values, just as Laura did.

ENDNOTES

[1] Laura Ingalls Wilder, *These Happy Golden Years*, HarperCollins Publishers, chapter "Nellie Oleson."
[2] Laura Ingalls Wilder, *The Long Winter*, HarperCollins Publishers, chapter "Cap Garland."
[3] John F. Case, "Let's Visit Mrs. Wilder," *Missouri Ruralist*, February 20, 1918.
[4] Laura Ingalls Wilder, *Missouri Ruralist*, September 5, 1917.
[5] Dan L. White, *Laura Ingalls' Friends Remember Her*, Ashley Preston Publishing, chapter two, "Interview with Nava Austin."
[6] Dan L. White, *Devotionals with Laura*, Ashley Preston Publishing, Prologue
[7] *Laura Ingalls' Friends Remember Her*, chapter seven, "Interview with Neta Seal."
[8] *Laura Ingalls' Friends Remember Her*, chapter two.
[9] *Missouri Ruralist*, November 20, 1919.
[10] Judith Thurmond, *The New Yorker* magazine, August 10, 2009.
[11] John E. Miller, *Becoming Laura Ingalls Wilder*, Thorndike Press, chapter six, "Turning to Autobiography, 1923-32."
[12] Laura Ingalls Wilder, Edited by Roger Lea MacBride, *West from Home*, Harper & Row Publishers, August 25, 1915.
[13] *Little House on the Prairie*, Show Summary, http://www.tv.com/little-house-on-the-prairie/show/732/summary.html.
[14] Bonanza: Scenery of the Ponderosa, Cast Biographies, Michael Landon, http://ponderosascenery.homestead.com/files/castbios/joe.html.
[15] Melissa Sue Anderson, *The Way I See It*, Globe Pequot publishers, chapter one, "Too Well Fed and a Seven-Year Contract."
[16] Cast Biographies, Michael Landon
[17] *Missouri Ruralist*, November 5, 1917.
[18] Laura Ingalls Wilder, *On the Banks of Plum Creek*, HarperCollins Publishers, chapter "The Christmas Horses."
[19] *Little House in the Big Woods, On the Banks of Plum Creek, By the Shores of Silver Lake, The Long Winter, Little Town on the Prairie, These Happy Golden Years, First Four Years*.
[20] *Little House on the Prairie* (TV Series), Wikipedia, http://en.wikipedia.org/wiki/Little_House_on_the_Prairie_%28TV_series%29.

[21] John F. Case, February 20, 1918.
[22] *Missouri Ruralist*, November 5, 1917.
[23] *Missouri Ruralist*, Jan 5, 1917.
[24] Season 1, Episode 5, http://www.tv.com/shows/little-house-on-the-prairie/trivia/.
[25] Laura Ingalls Wilder and Rose Wilder Lane, edited by William Anderson, *A Little House Sampler*, HarperCollins Publishers, chapter "Grandpa's Fiddle."
[26] Wilder Days 2012, http://www.wilderdays-mansfieldmo.com/blog/about-2/.
[27] Peter and Eliza Ingalls, http://www.liwfrontiergirl.com/peter.html.
[28] Laura Ingalls Wilder, *Little Town on the Prairie*, HarperCollins Publishers, chapter "Name Cards."
[29] Laura Ingalls Wilder, *Farmer Boy*, HarperCollins Publishers, chapter one, "School Days."
[30] *Missouri Ruralist*, January 5, 1920.
[31] *Laura Ingalls' Friends Remember Her*, chapter 3, "Interview with Peggy and Erman Dennis."
[32] Dean Butler Interview, Prairie Fans.com, http://www.pioneerontheprairie.com/dean.htm.
[33] Dan L. White, *Laura Ingalls Wilder's Most Inspiring Writings*, Ashley Preston Publishing, article 48.
[34] Dan L. White, *Laura's Love Story*, Ashley Preston Publishing, Prologue.
[35] *Little House on the Prairie*, chapter, "Going West."
[36] *New World Encyclopedia*, "Laura Ingalls Wilder," http://www.newworldencyclopedia.org/entry/%20Laura_Ingalls_Wilder.
[37] Keystone Area Historical Society, "Carrie Ingalls Swanzey," http://www.keystonechamber.com/kahs/carrieingalls.html.
[38] Ibid.
[39] Roosevelt Inn History, http://www.rosyinn.com/1320.html.
[40] Laura Ingalls Wilder, Frontier Girl, "Carrie Ingalls," http://www.liwfrontiergirl.com/.
[41] http://www.laurasprairiehouse.com/tvseries/season5ep102.html.
[42] PopEater Staff, "Husband of 'Little House' Star Kills Self," June 10, 2009, http://www.popeater.com/2009/06/10/little-house-on-the-prairie-suicide/.
[43] Little House on the Prairie, chapter "The House on the Prairie."
[44] Little House on the Prairie, chapter "Mr. Edwards Meets Santa Claus."
[45] Walnut Grove History, http://www.walnutgrove.org/wghistory.htm.

[46] Welcome to Walnut Grove, MN, History-City of Walnut Grove, http://www.walnutgrovemn.org/Community/History/.
[47] Ibid.
[48] Ibid.
[49] Laura Ingalls Wilder, *By the Shores of Silver Lake*, HarperCollins Publishers, chapter "On the Pilgrim Way."
[50] *The New York Times*, August, 15, 1878, http://query.nytimes.com/mem/archive-free/pdf?res=F10B1EF73E58157B93C7A81783D85F4C8784F9.
[51] Annual Report of the Commissioner of Indian Affairs to the Secretary of the Interior, The Year 1878, http://www.archive.org/stream/1878annualreport00unitrich#page/34/mode/2up.
[52] Laura Ingalls Wilder, unpublished manuscript *Pioneer Girl*.
[53] "When the Skies Turned to Black: The Grasshopper Plague of 1875," A study of the intersection of history and genealogy, http://www.hearthstonelegacy.com/when-the-skies-turned-to-black-the_locust-plague-of-1875.htm.
[54] *The History of Henry and St. Clair County, Missouri*, 1883, National Historical Company, St. Joseph, Mo., author and publishers, http://archive.org/details/historyofhenryst00nati.
[55] Jeffrey A. Lockwood, "Voices from the Past: What We Can Learn from the Rocky Mountain Locust," http://www.hearthstonelegacy.com/when-the-skies-turned-to-black-the_locust-plague-of-1875.htm.
[56] *On the Banks of Plum Creek*, chapter "Rain."
[57] Laura Ingalls Wilder, *The First Four Years*, HarperCollins Publishers, chapter "The First Year."
[58] Charlotte Stewart (Miss Beadle) Exclusive Interview, http://www.pioneerontheprairie.com/cs.htm.
[59] *On the Banks of Plum Creek*, chapter "School."
[60] *Pioneer Girl* manuscript.
[61] Ibid.
[62] William Anderson, *Laura Ingalls Wilder: The Iowa Story*, Laura Ingalls Wilder Park and Museum, 1989.
[63] *Pioneer Girl* manuscript.
[64] Ibid.
[65] The Turnbaugh Twins Fansite, http://www.zunshine.com/turnbaugh/biography.html.
[66] Laura's Listography, TV Guide's list of TV's Top 100 Episodes of all time, listography.com/action/list?uid=5148184796&lid=6529225895.

[67] *Pioneer Girl* manuscript.
[68] Mary Ingalls, picture in the public domain, http://en.wikipedia.org/wiki/File:MaryIngalls_1.jpg#filelinks.
[69] *By the Shores of Silver Lake*, chapter "Unexpected Visitor."
[70] Melissa Sue Anderson, http://www.imdb.com/name/nm0000757/.
[71] Rodney Ho, Radio and TV Talk, "Interview with Melissa Sue Anderson," http://blogs.ajc.com/radio-tv-talk/2010/05/05/interview-with-melissa-sue-anderson-mary-on-little-house-on-the-prairie-coming-to-atlanta-510-511/
[72] Ibid.
[73] Wikipedia, "List of *Little House on the Prairie*" episodes, http://en.wikipedia.org/wiki/List_of_Little_House_on_the_Prairie_episodes.
[74] *Pioneer Girl* manuscript.
[75] Ibid.
[76] Dan L. White, *Big Bible Lessons from Laura Ingalls' Little Books*, Ashley Preston Publishing, Lesson two, Bible Marriage.
[77] Dan L. White, *The Long, Hard Winter of 1880-81: What was it really like?*, Ashley Preston Publishing, chapter one, "The Black, Hard, Long, Snow Winter."
[78] Ibid., chapter four, "Blizzard at School."
[79] *Pioneer Girl* manuscript.
[80] *The Long, Hard Winter of 1880-81*, chapter eight, "The Long, Hard, Black, Snow, Flood, Whatever Winter."
[81] *Little Town on the Prairie*, chapter "The Necessary Cat."
[82] Mac-Ale, Reviewer for "Centennial" episode of *Little House on the Prairie*, comment, http://www.tv.com/shows/little-house-on-the-prairie/centennial-63918/.
[83] *Missouri Ruralist*, July 5, 1918.
[84] *The Long, Hard Winter of 1880-81*, chapter two, "The Awful Autumn Blizzard."
[85] *These Happy Golden Years*, chapter "Wedding Plans."
[86] *Pioneer Girl* manuscript.
[87] Ibid.
[88] Ibid.
[89] Definitive Laura Ingalls Wilder & Little House on the Prairie, "Eliza Jane Wilder," Biography, http://www.laurasprairiehouse.com/family/elizajanewilder.html.
[90] *Pioneer Girl* manuscript.
[91] *Little Town on the Prairie*, chapter "Name Cards."

[92] Ibid.
[93] *These Happy Golden Years*, chapter "One Week."
[94] *Pioneer Girl* manuscript.
[95] *Missouri Ruralist*, December 15, 1924.
[96] *These Happy Golden Years*, chapter "Cold Ride."
[97] Prairie Fans.com, *De Smet News*, http://www.pioneerontheprairie.com/liw_history.htm.
[98] *First Four Year*, chapter "The First Year."
[99] *Laura's Love Story*, chapter four, "Growing Together."
[100] *Laura Ingalls' Friends Remember Her*, chapter three, "Peggy and Erman Dennis."
[101] *Laura's Love Story*, chapter four, "Growing Together."
[102] *Laura Ingalls' Friends Remember Her*, chapter two.
[103] *The Long Winter*, chapter "Not Really Hungry."
[104] Big woods cabin, Kansas cabin, dugout, house by Plum Creek, hotel in Burr Oak, rented house in Burr Oak, built house in Burr Oak, surveyors' house by Silver Lake, homestead cabin, store building in De Smet and house on third street, and perhaps one in Missouri.
[105] *The Way I See It*, chapter one, "Too Well Fed and a Seven-Year Contract."
[106] *Missouri Ruralist*, September 20, 1916.
[107] Jerry Buck, the *Palm Beach Post*, "Dean Butler Hits it Big in New Shot at 'Little House'," July 12, 1982, http://news.google.com/newspapers?id=eqImAAAAIBAJ&sjid=7wEGAAAAIBAJ&pg=3049,128532&dq=dean-butler&hl=en.
[108] *Missouri Ruralist*, February 5, 1917.
[109] Larry King Live, CNN, Transcript of interview with Alison Arngrim, April 24, 2004, http://transcripts.cnn.com/TRANSCRIPTS/0404/27/lkl.00.html.
[110] *On the Banks of Plum Creek*, chapter "Nellie Oleson."
[111] *The Long Winter*, chapter "Pa Goes to Volga."
[112] *On the Banks of Plum Creek*, chapter "Nellie Oleson."
[113] Classic TV Hits, http://www.classictvhits.com/tvratings/index.htm.
[114] *People*, "Happy Birthday Mr. President: a Sampler of Great Late Bloomers Proves Life Can Begin at 70," Vol. 15, No. 5, February 9, 1981, http://www.people.com/people/archive/article/0,,20078565,00.html.
[115] *Missouri Ruralist*, November 15, 1922.

Other books by Dan L. White

Information available at danlwhitebooks.com
Email at mail@danlwhitebooks.com.
Find us on Facebook at Dan L White Books.

The Jubilee Principle
God's Plan for Economic Freedom

WND Books, available at wndbooks.com.

–examines the economic "long wave", a boom-and-bust cycle that happens roughly twice a century in free economies, and parallels the wisdom of the fifty-year Jubilee cycle in the Bible. *The Jubilee Principle* shows how God designed Israel's society with the Sabbath, festivals, land sabbath and Jubilee year. How would it be to live a whole life under that system? *The Jubilee Principle* points the way to true security.

Laura's Love Story
The lifetime love of Laura Ingalls and Almanzo Wilder

Real love is sometimes stronger than the romance of fiction. Laura and Almanzo's love is such a story. From an unwanted beau – Almanzo – to a beautiful romance; from the heart wrenching tragedy of losing their home and little boy to heart felt passion; from trials that most do not endure to a love that endured for a lifetime –

Laura's Love Story is the true account of two young people who lived through the most trying troubles to form the most lasting love.

Better than fiction, truer than life, this is the love story that put the jollity in Laura's stories and is the final happy ending to her Little House® books.

Laura Ingalls' Friends Remember Her
Memories from Laura's Ozark Home

– contains memories from Laura and Almanzo's close friends, Ozarkers who knew them around their home town of Mansfield, Missouri. We chat with these folks, down home and close up, about their good friends Laura and Almanzo.

Laura also joins in our chats because we include long swatches of her magazine writings on whatever subject is at hand. It's almost as if she's there talking with us. Her thoughts on family and little farms and what-not are more interesting than almost anybody you've ever talked to.

Plus the book contains discussions of –
- how Laura's Ozark life made her happy books possible;
- what made Laura's books so happy;
- whether her daughter Rose wrote Laura's books;
- and Laura's last, lonely little house.

Laura Ingalls' Friends Remember Her includes –
- her friends' recollections;
- Laura's writings from her magazine articles;
- and fresh discussions of Laura's happy books and her life.

Laura's readers should find these insights into the Little House life interesting and uplifting.

The Long, Hard Winter of 1880-81 –What was it Really Like?

Laura Ingalls Wilder's classic novel *The Long Winter* tells the riveting story of the winter of 1880-81. She wrote of three day blizzards, forty ton trains stuck in the snow, houses buried in snowdrifts and a town that nearly starved.

Just how much of her story was fact, and how much was fiction? Was that winter really that bad, or was it just a typical old time winter stretched a bit to make a good tale?

Author Dan L. White examines the reality of the long, hard winter. Was Laura's story just fiction, or was that one winter stranger than fiction?

Devotionals with Laura
Laura Ingalls' Favorite Bible Selections;
What they meant in her life, what they might mean in yours –

Laura Ingalls Wilder was a wonderful writer and an eager Bible reader. After her death a list of her most cherished Bible selections was found in her Bible. *Devotionals with Laura* discusses these Bible passages, including:

- How they might have fit in with Laura's life;
- What they might mean in our lives;
- How they affected the Little House books.

When Laura said that she read a certain passage at a time of crisis or discouragement in her life, what events might have caused her to do that? When was she in a crisis? When was she discouraged? What did she say in her writings about such a time?

We include excerpts from Laura's articles where she talked about such events. When we have done these *Devotionals with Laura*, meditated on the passages she meditated on, considered her words for life's critical times, and taken in deeply the very words of Almighty God, then we can begin to understand how Laura's little Bible helped shape the Little House® books.

Laura Ingalls Wilder's Most Inspiring Writings
Notes and Setting by Dan L. White

These sparkling works of Laura Ingalls Wilder came **before** she wrote her famous book *Little House on the Prairie*, from which the television show came. The eight other books she wrote tell of her life as a girl on the American frontier between about 1870 and 1889. But years before writing these books, she wrote articles about small farms, country living and just living life for the *Missouri Ruralist* magazine. *Laura Ingalls Wilder's Most Inspiring Writings* is a collection of forty-eight of the most interesting and uplifting of these writings.

Within Laura's words are gems of down to earth wisdom. Amazingly, most of her comments mean just as much today as when she wrote them. These writings give us her philosophy of life and are the seed stock of Laura's prairie books.

Big Bible Lessons from Laura Ingalls' Little Books

The Little House® books by Laura Ingalls Wilder are lovable, classic works of literature. They contain no violence and no vulgarities, yet they captivate young readers and whole families with their warmth and interest.

They tell the life of young Laura Ingalls, who grew up on the American frontier after the Civil War. Laura was part of a conservative Christian family, and they lived their lives based on certain unchanging values – drawn from the Bible.

Big Bible Lessons from Laura Ingalls' Little Books examines the Bible principles that are the foundation of Laura's writing, the Ingalls family, and the Little House® books. Not directly stated in words, they were firmly declared in the everyday lives of the Ingalls family. While you enjoy Laura's wonderful books, this book and these Bible lessons will help you and your family also grow spiritually from them.

Reading along with Laura Ingalls in the Big Wisconsin Woods

Little House in the Big Woods fans can now enjoy that beloved story a little more.

Reading along with Laura Ingalls in the Big Wisconsin Woods delves a little deeper into Pa's stories about panthers and bears and honey bee trees, the dance at Grandpa's house, going into the town of Pepin, and the other goings-on in Laura's book.

Read along and discover how Laura wrote her book and how the times were, in and beyond the Ingalls' cabin. Most of all, you can join in the warmth and wonderful family life that is tenderly talked about in Laura's book and in this book.

Reading along with Laura Ingalls at her Kansas Prairie Home

Little House on the Prairie is the most famous of all the great books by Laura Ingalls Wilder. There she tells how her family traveled to Kansas and built a log house, how Pa almost died digging a well, how they were almost burned out by a prairie wildfire, and how they faced possible attack from wolves and Indians.

Reading Along with Laura Ingalls at her Kansas Prairie Home goes along with that book, chapter by chapter, event by event –

and tells more about how it really was – there in 1870 on that Kansas prairie.

Little House on the Prairie deserves more than just a quick read. Such a beloved book stirs thought, reflection and remembering. *Reading Along with Laura Ingalls at her Kansas Prairie Home* does that. Read along with Laura, laugh along with Laura, live along with Laura as we search out the times and spirit of these hardy pioneers. Join in as we stretch out your enjoyment of Laura's book, deepen your understanding of her character, and increase your affection for her wonderful family.

"Oh Charles!"

Homeschool Happenings, Happenstance & Happiness
A Light Look at Homeschool Life

Homeschool pioneers Margie and Dan White reflect on their homeschool experiences from 1976 until today. With *Homeschool Helpers*, they have held hundreds of homeschool activities and have put out a quarter million words of encouragement. This book includes the top tenth of those writings, everything from homeschooling in the world today to unforgettable family episodes. Such as –

"Most people do not see themselves as part of history. If you are a Christian homeschool family, you are part of one of the great religious movements in the history of America, perhaps the greatest. Just as God put the Jews back in the Holy Land, just as He is drawing some Jews to follow Christ, so He is calling you to follow the Messiah directly."

"With no institutions supporting it, and all of them opposing it, why in the world did homeschooling grow by perhaps 20% a year?"

"We taught all our five kids to read, starting at about age two. We had no idea that they were not "ready to learn." "

This book is about family, faith and fun – Homeschool happenings, happenstance, and happiness!

Tebows' Homeschooled! Should You?
How Homeschooling put God back in Education!

Tim Tebow is the world's most famous modern day homeschooler. His parents, Pam and Bob Tebow, homeschooled all five of their children. The intense attention on Tim has also put a spotlight on homeschooling. Although practically everyone in the country now knows about homeschooling, the movement still educates only a few percent of the overall student population. Most people are far more familiar with the factory approach to education than this method of individual tutoring.

Tim Tebow's homeschool education was typical of homeschooling in a number of ways. In some ways, of course, his experience was unique. Yet even in that uniqueness he typifies homeschooling, because homeschooling excels with uniqueness. Therefore, there is much to learn about homeschooling in general by looking at Tim Tebow's homeschooling. In this book, we try to draw out those lessons.

School Baals
How an old idol with a new name sneaked into your school

If you believe in the God of the Bible, that is religion and can't be taught in the government schools.

If you don't believe in the God of the Bible, that is not religion and can be taught in the government schools.

That is also one of the biggest deceptions ever foisted on any people in all of human history.

Idolatry is not just the worship of an idol, but the exalting of the human spirit against its creator. The same human nature that built Baal and made Molech created the anti-God deception that is taught to nine out of ten young people in America.

School Baals reveals this idolatry in all its duplicity and destruction, and tells you what you can do about it.

Wifely Wisdom for Sometimes Foolish Husbands
From Laura Ingalls to Almanzo and Abigail to Nabal

A Christian wife may be caught between a rock and a hard place. The rock is Christ, the spiritual rock who commands wives to be submissive to their husbands; and the hard place is the husband, who sometimes has less than perfect wisdom. *Wifely Wisdom for Sometimes Foolish Husbands* discusses the pickle of a wife being submissive but still sharing her wisdom with a husband during his few and far-between foolish moments. Such examples include Laura Ingalls sharing her insights with her husband Almanzo Wilder; Ma and Pa Ingalls; and Abigail and Nabal, whose very name meant fool.

This is a sprightly look at a serious subject, when marriage is under attack from all sides as never before. If a wife can share basic wisdom with her husband when he acts like Nabal, then they may save their marriage and rescue their family from destruction. Laura and Almanzo shared good times and bad times, through chucked churns and hot lid lifters, times when she spoke and times when she didn't, times when he listened and times when he didn't, and through all that their marriage lasted for sixty-three years. *Wifely Wisdom for Sometimes Foolish Husbands* may add a few years, or decades, or a lifetime, to your marriage.

Daring to Love like God
Marriage as a Spiritual Union

The Love Dare© program, made famous in the movie Fireproof©, was for people whose marriages had problems, to dare them to take steps to better those marriages. Daring to Love like God is the next step, for people with good marriages, who are not about to split, who love God and each other, and who want to grow to become a true spiritual union.

This is one of the great miracles in creation: two people, with different abilities, personalities and wants, who become one, with each other and with God. If you want to be challenged to the very best marriage, Daring to Love like God leads you up that path.

Life Lessons from Jane Austen's Pride and Prejudice
From her book, her characters and her Bible

Seven characters in *Pride and Prejudice* –

- Mr. George Wickham, with a most pleasing appearance;
- Miss Jane Bennet, who thought ill of no one and who spoke against no ills;
- Miss Charlotte Lucas, who married for position and got only what she sought;
- Mr. William Collins, whose humble abode was so very close to Rosings Park;
- Miss Elizabeth Bennet, with her consuming search for a man of character;
- and Mr. Fitzwilliam Darcy, who helped her find him –

These seven characters in *Pride and Prejudice* present seven aspects of human nature and the consequent complications of obtaining character, in portrayals that were carefully planned and scripted by Miss Austen. *Life Lessons from Jane Austen's Pride and Prejudice* examines Jane's purposeful plan, searching out the depths of her memorable personalities, and seeking the profundity of her meaningful lessons in life, in morality, and in young love.

Fans of both the *Pride and Prejudice* novel and the movies who appreciated Miss Austen's strong moral values will appreciate this easy flowing study of her comedic characters and her Christian character, making a great love story even better.

Printed in Great Britain
by Amazon